THE RAILWAYS OF EAST YORKSHIRE

C. T. Goode

THE OAKWOOD PRESS

List of Abbreviations Found in the Text

dmu	diesel multiple unit
DVLR	Derwent Valley Light Railway
GCR	Great Central Railway
GER	Great Eastern Railway
GNER	Great North of England Railway
GNR	Great Northern Railway
GWR	Great Western Railway
H&BR	Hull and Barnsley Railway
H&HR	Hull and Hornsea Railway
H&SR	Hull and Selby Railway
L&YR	Lancashire and Yorkshire Railway
LMSR	London, Midland and Scottish Railway
LNER	London and North Eastern Railway
MS&LR	Manchester, Sheffield and Lincolnshire Railway
MR	Midland Railway
M&DR	Malton and Driffield Railway
NER	North Eastern Railway
SB&WRJc.R	Selby, Bridlington and West Riding Junction Railway
SHLR	Sand Hutton Light Railway
SYR	South Yorkshire Railway
SO	Saturdays only
SX	Except Saturdays
ThO	Thursdays only
TuO	Tuesdays only
XP	express
Y&NMR	York and North Midland Railway

ISBN 0 85361 280 3

CONTENTS

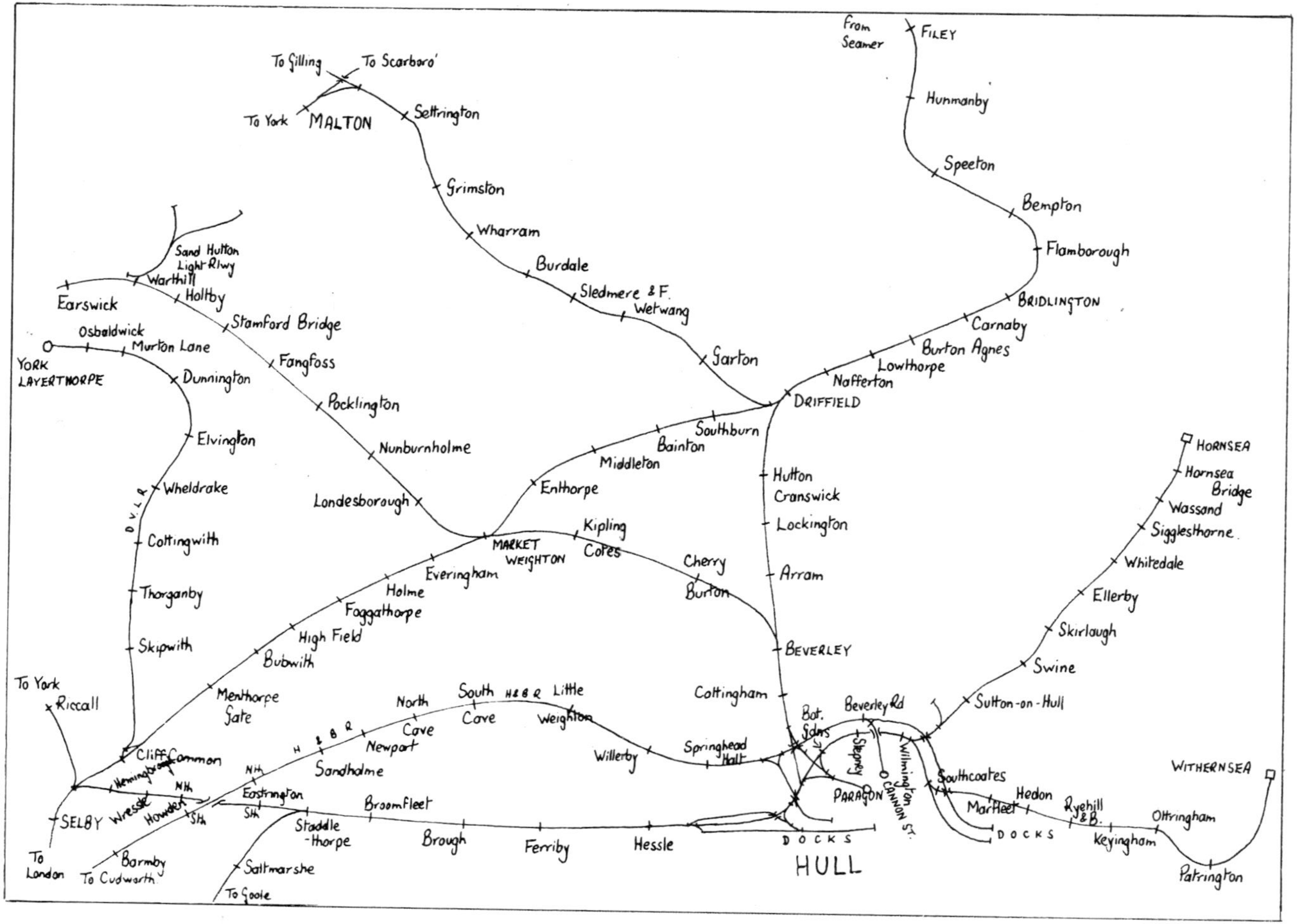
From Seamer
FILEY
Hunmanby
Speeton
Bempton
Flamborough
BRIDLINGTON
Carnaby
Burton Agnes
Lowthorpe
Nafferton
DRIFFIELD
To Gilling
To Scarboro'
To York
MALTON
Settrington
Grimston
Wharram
Burdale
Sledmere & F.
Wetwang
Garton
Sand Hutton Light Rlwy
Warthill
Earswick
Holtby
Stamford Bridge
Fangfoss
Pocklington
Nunburnholme
Londesborough
Osbaldwick
Murton Lane
YORK LAYERTHORPE
Dunnington
Elvington
D.V.L.R
Wheldrake
Cottingwith
Thorganby
Skipwith
Southburn
Bainton
Middleton
Enthorpe
Hutton Cranswick
Lockington
Arram
BEVERLEY
MARKET WEIGHTON
Kipling Cotes
Cherry Burton
Everingham
Holme
Foggathorpe
High Field
Bubwith
Menthorpe Gate
HORNSEA
Hornsea Bridge
Wassand
Sigglesthorne
Whitedale
Ellerby
Skirlaugh
Swine
Sutton-on-Hull
To York
Riccall
Cliff Common
Hemingbrough
Nth
SELBY
Wressle
Howden
Sth
To London
Barmby
To Cudworth
H & B R
North Cave
South Cave
Little Weighton
Newport
Sandholme
Eastrington
Willerby
Springhead Halt
Cottingham
Bot. Gdns
Beverley Rd
Stepney
Wilmington
CANNON ST.
PARAGON
Staddle-thorpe
Broomfleet
Brough
Ferriby
Hessle
Saltmarshe
To Goole
DOCKS
HULL
Southcoates
Marfleet
Hedon
Ryehill & B.
Keyingham
Ottringham
Patrington
WITHERNSEA

Foreword

The old East Riding of Yorkshire, before it became North Humberside and other names besides, spent its entire existence largely unknown to the general public, who were unaware of its impressive streams and Wolds which have a rounded, unruffled and timeless serenity of their own. Here the sky is always bluer and the rain, when it falls, is clean and bears little pollution. To the holidaymaker seeking sandy beaches, there were those station names to muse over on the way; Driffield, Market Weighton and Bubwith among many, the latter name becoming something of a joke to South Yorkshire folk for some unexplained reason. Hull, or rather Kingston-upon-Hull if one is to be correct, lies at the south of it all as a fiercely proud industrial oasis destined always to be at the end of a branch, itself the originator of yet more branches which end up at vaguely heard of places somewhere on the coast.

The confines of the East Riding were small, and yet as this book will show, the railway activities here were lively and diverse, from the frequent clashing of level crossing gates all along the last lap to Bridlington on a busy holiday Saturday, to the platforms at Wassand waiting patiently for their weekly stopping train.

I have attempted to trace in some detail the railway routes included here and to present the social and economic development of the system in a readable way, untrammeled as far as possible by Acts of Parliament and their dates which can be tedious. These I have kept on a short rein. For the earnest seeker after detail there are excellent general works by Messrs. Tomlinson and Allen on the North Eastern Railway, also the two volume History of the Hull and Barnsley Railway which contains the researches of many knowledgeable heads.

I should like to acknowledge the assistance given to me by Mrs. Boddington of the County Record Office in Beverley, and to those railwaymen and others who have been both informative and encouraging.

Anlaby, Hull. C. Tony Goode, B.A.

HULL & BARNSLEY RAILWAY.

Every Thursday and Saturday,

Until Further Notice,

COOK'S CHEAP DAY EXCURSIONS TO

SHEFFIELD,

With Bookings on Saturdays for **2** or **3** days.

From	dep.	dep.	To SHEFFIELD.	
	a.m.	a.m.	Day Trip Fare.	2 or 3 Days on Saturdays only.
HULL—				
Cannon Street	7 0	9 40	**2/9**	**4/9**
Beverley Road	7 4	9 44		
HOWDEN	7 50	10 24		
Sheffield ... ... arr.	9 22	11 45		

The Return Train will leave Sheffield at 6-58 p.m. or 8-28 p.m. each day.

Passengers taking tickets at the higher fares must return by ordinary train leaving Sheffield at 6-58 p.m. or 8-28 p.m. on Week-days, and on Sundays at 3-34 p.m.

Every Thursday, Saturday and Sunday,

Until further notice, Cook's Cheap Return Tickets to

LITTLE WEIGHTON, SOUTH CAVE & NORTH CAVE,

Available to return from either Station on day of issue; and to

DRAX and KIRK SMEATON,

Will be issued as under:—

From	Times of Starting.				Return Fares, Third Class.		
	Week-Days.			Sundays.	LITTLE WEIGHTON, SOUTH CAVE and NORTH CAVE.	DRAX.	KIRK SMEATON.
HULL—	p.m.	p.m.	p.m.	By any ordinary stopping train in each direction.	Third Class.	Third Class.	Third Class.
Cannon Street ...	12 30	1 25	3 0		**1/-**	**1/3**	**1/9**
Beverley Road ...	12 34	1 29	3 4				

NOTE.—Bookings to Drax and Kirk Smeaton by 12-30 p.m. train. Bookings to Little Weighton, South and North Cave, by any of the three trains named.

BICYCLES.—Bicycle Tickets, at owner's risk are issued to Excursionists from Hull to **KIRK SMEATON** at **1/-** each return when properly labelled.

Children under 3 years of age, free; above 3 and under 12, half-fares. The tickets are not transferable, and are available by the trains herein-named only. No luggage allowed to passengers taking day or half-day trip tickets. Passengers holding long-date tickets are allowed 60 lbs. of luggage free, under their own care, for which the Company will not be responsible.

NOTE.—The Tickets are only available to and from the Stations named above, and passengers alighting at any other Station will forfeit their tickets and be required to pay the full ordinary fare.

Should the Company consider it necessary or desirable, from any cause, to alter or cancel these arrangements, they reserve to themselves the right to do so.

Chapter 1

The Early Days

East Yorkshire remains in many ways much as it always was, in spite of the relentless pace of modern life and the whims of Government which have brought about new regional divisions such as North Wolds and North Humberside, which are purely artificial and only serve to split up what is quite a distinctive area stretching from Filey in the north down to Hull and along the Humber and Ouse to Selby in the west. Selby was to play quite a part in the early development of the East Riding and its opening out, as indeed was Goole to the south west, which acted as a competitive stimulus to Hull in getting rail communication established. Hull was already a well-established seaport and industrial centre long before the railway came. The town became a port in the reign of Edward I and shipped most of the goods manufactured in Yorkshire which were destined for overseas, these being brought by water from York. The waterways were the prime movers, since the roads were sketchy, apart from the important Via Regia striking northwards from Hessle to Beverley after having reached the southern shore of the Humber through Lincolnshire. Apart from the obvious artery from the west which the Humber provided, and that route south along the Trent, there was the river Hull from Driffield and Beverley in the north. Crossing of the wide and often treacherous Humber could be made originally by the Royal Ferry between Barton and Hessle, though this became expensive after a time, and eventually a ½d ferry was instituted in the reign of Edward II between Hull and Barton, much as nowadays, though alas no longer ½d, and one of the oldest river crossings in the country.

With the Turnpikes and Enclosures Act of the 1780s roads throughout the land were improved and coaches and carriages became more numerous. Traffic to and from the East Riding went via Selby and Hull, the London traffic being conveyed across the water to Barton and on to the south via Lincolnshire. Coaches also ran between Hull and Doncaster and Hull and Selby. Competition on the latter route was offered by the steamboat 'Caledonia' which began to run to and from Selby in 1815.

McTurk's 'History of the Railways into Hull' gives details of interesting and often amusing advertisements for coach services in the 1850s, including those serving a choice of two routes between Hull and Bridlington and Scarborough, one concern operating the 'British Queen' along the Brandesburton road, the last six miles of which, being close to the seaside, were 'delightfully beautiful'. The competing firm, running 'Magna Charta' by way of Beverley and Driffield, simply extolled their route as being universally well-known and shot down their competitors as follows:

'The Sea (has) made such a dreadful havoc of the Brandesburton road during the last few years as to render it dangerous travelling that way, being, for five or six miles, quite at the edge of the cliff.'

The 'Rapid' was a coach of 1835 which left Hull at 6.45 a.m. and ran by way of the Caves and Howden, Booth Ferry where half an hour was allowed for breakfast, Snaith, Huddersfield and Ashton, getting into Manchester at 7 p.m. The old ferry link to London was maintained by the Union Day coach promoters of Barton, Lincoln, Grantham and Leicester, whose vehicle connected with the packet for Hull, leaving Barton at 8 a.m. and running to Leicester via Lincoln, Grantham and Melton Mowbray. As the Midland Railway was to do in later years, it waxed eloquent over its connections available for the 'Man of Business' and the 'Tourist', and the advertising mentioned access to every place in the south, west and east, not forgetting Wales.

As already said, Goole was a form of stimulus to the promotion of positive land links with Hull, freeing it from its splendid isolation down the Humber estuary, and the young town suddenly developed as a result of the opening of a new canal between there and Ferrybridge, the goods, mainly woollens, leaving Goole and of course by-passing Hull on their way to continental ports.

Hull had already been considered as the proposed terminus of a new line, the Leeds and Hull Railway Company formed in December 1824, which constituted the third part of an eventual route from Liverpool to Hull, the Liverpool and Manchester Railway of Rainhill Trials fame having been opened in May 1825. Seeing the ease with which goods could be manoeuvred along the canal to Goole, the Yorkshire folk were not in any hurry to subscribe money to the L & H, so that the venture was in danger of lapsing. A compromise was hastily thought out and the L & H now became the Leeds and Selby Railway Company of March 1829, running along a freshly conceived route from a station in Marsh Lane, Leeds by a reasonably graded run of twenty miles to a riverside terminus at Selby, where it was intended that unfortunate Hull passengers should transfer to a steam packet for the rest of the way. The line had interesting engineering features in the 700yd. long tunnel just outside Marsh Lane, opened out in later years, and quite respectable cuttings and embankments in the Milford and Crossgates area.

The first official run was made in September 1834 along what was as yet a single track, the start being made at 6.30 a.m. behind the engine 'Nelson' which distinguished itself by slipping on the damp rails, bringing several times to a stand its load of 156 passengers in nine yellow coaches. Total running time for this first trip was three hours for the 20 miles, but in fairness it must be said that 'Nelson' managed the return journey in 76 minutes. Usually an hour was allowed for the twice daily run, the trains connecting with the Selby packets which promised further thrills by frequently grounding in the river, plenty of opportunities for this on the sinuous run of 33 miles which might take up to 5 hours.

Of the two terminals, that at Selby, was bigger with six tracks instead of four and with wooden buildings with roofs in bays. Here was to be found the neat idea of letting the roof water run down the inside of the hollow supporting columns to be collected for use. As was the practice at the time, the lines were connected by small turntables to facilitate the movement of the short vehicles by hand or horse power. At Selby one of the tracks ran out over the river on to a short jetty to reassure rail passengers that they had in fact reached the watery portion of their journey.

The Leeds and Selby Railway was therefore the first passenger line to penetrate eastwards from Leeds, and pre-dated the York and North Midland line from Normanton, on the North Midland from Derby to Leeds, by some five years. Where the two lines crossed at Milford, connections were put in from both north and south to the east, and passengers who desired to travel between Leeds and York could travel to a point just beyond the connections called York Jc, later Gascoigne Wood and change there.

At the northern end, and along the northern edge of the East Riding railway movements were astir, for when the Y & N M had reached York via Milford in June 1840, it was logical for another independent company with the grandiose title of the Great North of England to come southwards from Darlington and gain the York terminus by a rather laboured reversal. The NER seemed to like this sort of thing, as witness the awkward entry to the Whitby branch from Scarborough.

The Y & N M opened its line from York to Scarborough, with the branch from Rillington to Pickering, in July 1845. The course of the line ran mainly along the valley of the Derwent, a river which, to this day, persists in flowing in an ungeographical manner away from the sea. The first train on the York and Scarborough was composed of two engines and 35 coaches crammed with passengers holding free tickets, indeed almost a week of free travel whetted the appetite of the customers before business began. In York the branch trains had to perform a sort of billiards action, reversing in order to gain the terminus or leave it. Following the river as it did, the line was somewhat sinuous in character, especially between Malton and Strensall, and a noteworthy feature was a 400ft. timber viaduct over the river near Huttons Ambo, as well as the rather unpretentious but expensive bridge immediately outside York station which bore the line over the Ouse.

The people of Hull were, and still are, a placid folk and could tolerate much, yet it was becoming too much to have to suffer the fifty or so miles up and down the river to Selby when there was a chance of obtaining a railway which would be almost straight and level and which could lop off 20 miles and hours of journey time at one stroke.

'A gentleman recently going from Hull to Leeds by the Steam Packet was informed that the vessel would leave the Pier precisely at Eight o' clock a.m. On attending at that hour it appeared that a London steamer had just arrived, having goods on board for Leeds. The Selby Packet was detained in order to take them forward, and did not actually leave Hull before Ten o' clock, two hours after the time fixed. In consequence of this delay, the Steamer had to encounter on her passage strong freshes in the river, and did not reach Selby until about Four o' clock p.m.; the journey to Leeds by coach was not completed before seven o' clock in the evening, the entire day having been thus consumed in effecting a journey which, by the projected railway, will be accomplished in Three Hours.' (McTurk).

A committee was formed made up of local businessmen headed by Mr. Henry Broadley and backed by a capital amount of £350,000. Two routes were proposed; both took the same direct course to Brough, the original turning into the Wolds and running through a tunnel rather in the manner of the later Hull and Barnsley Railway, to reach Cottingham and enter the city from the north. However, the present line of route via Hessle was adopted, skirting the Humber shore, avoiding hills and arriving at a terminus by the Humber Dock.

Mr McTurk gives full details of the building in his book, and describes the train shed as follows:

'A very spacious, lofty, light, and, for its purpose, handsome structure. It is 170ft. long by 72ft. wide, and of the extreme height of about 40ft. The roof is supported by twenty-two iron columns. This building is lighted by twenty-two windows, and the west end is perfectly open. On each side are raised platforms twelve feet wide and extending the entire length of the building for the convenience of stepping in and out of the passengers' carriages.'

The line was opened on 1st. July 1840 and was well received by the townsfolk in the customary manner, four trains leaving Hull at midday to the accompaniment of pouring rain and a barrage of speeches, one by no less a person than George Hudson. The run over the flat and straight line of 31 miles was completed in approximately two hours, and the return journeys were made in sunshine, this latter stimulating the drivers to push their mounts a little harder and cover the distance in the round hour. A Dinner was held in the Hull Goods Warehouse and more speeches were heard.

At the Selby end the line had to cross the Ouse, and managed this by means of a cast iron bridge of 190ft. in length with two hand-operated opening flaps, each of 93 tons weight to give a river opening of 45ft. It was claimed that the operation could be completed in one minute by such muscle power, and the bridge survived in situ to carry the additional East Coast Main Line traffic until it was superceded.

The permanent way was sturdily constructed with 63lb. rails on tranverse sleepers and 55lb. flat bottomed rails on longitudinal sleepers using chairs to secure them. The Opening Day notice offered a service of four trains each way, leaving Hull at 7a.m., 10a.m., 3p.m. and 6p.m. for Leeds and York with good connections off the first three. The third class single fare to Leeds was 4s.6d. which was quite expensive for the time. All trains stopped at the stations of Hessle (4 miles), Ferriby (7 miles), Brough (10 miles), Staddlethorpe (16 miles), Eastrington (19 miles), Howden & Bubwith (20 miles) and Cliffe, sometimes spelt Cliff (28 miles), before Selby.

The local newspaper of the day was very enthusiastic about the new line which was, after all, a significant development in the communications of the whole area, and dilated on the fine skew bridges, over the cutting of 36ft. in depth at Hessle, near the Humber Bridge site today, where could also be seen the Station House of white brick, hidden in the same cutting. Mention was made too of the straight stretch of 18 miles which it considered would eventually be something of a record even in those days. Ferriby appeared to have no Station House at the outset, the next being at Brough, 'the handsomest on the Line'. Here the old York to Lincoln road made by the Romans was crossed and the building of the line produced enough relics to fill a wagon. Broomfleet was yet to come into the railway picture, but the nearby bridge of 70ft. span over the Market Weighton canal is mentioned, its virtual twin being that over the Derwent, the same perverse river mentioned earlier near Wressle or Wressel, where stands the ruin of the Duke of Northumberland's castle. The passenger's destination, Selby, is described as 'convenient', and through passengers for Leeds and York were invited to keep their seats 'for forward conveyance.'

Business grew, and a feature of the operation was the running of excursions to the Hull Tuesday markets, with a free ride back on the 3p.m. if one travelled out on the 9a.m. On one Tuesday in 1844 some 7,800 people used special trains offering the return excursion facility from Leeds to Hull. Apparently the Hull and Selby Railway did a good business in second-hand headgear which had blown off the heads of customers using the inferior open-air accommodation.

After five years of independent working, the H & S R was placed under the aegis of the Y & N M in August 1845, thus sowing the seeds of eventual monopoly by the N E R which was to cause great concern to the citizens of Hull. However, this course of action was an alternative to a union with the Liverpool and Manchester company, which would have brought the port of Hull into open competition with Goole, a town already favoured by the latter company.

Chapter 2

First Lines to Market Weighton

Trains between Hull and York had been running, as nowadays, via Selby up to the opening of the more direct link between Beverley and Market Weighton in May 1865, to join up with the York-Market Weighton service started 20 years earlier.

The York to Market Weighton line was completed and opened in October 1847, branching off from the York to Scarborough line at Bootham Jc., whence it ran to the first station at Earswick, originally named Huntington. The NER avoided giving stations names similar to stations elsewhere; the next station, Stockton, had to be changed for obvious reasons of similarity, and the name Warthill was chosen, becoming a little famous in railway circles because it was the starting point of the little Sand Hutton Light Railway. Warthill was also the first place in the country to receive lifting barriers to replace crossing gates.

From this point the line turned to run due south-east towards Market Weighton, serving several stations on the way which are again mainly of interest because of their nomenclature. Holtby was a slightly later addition of 1848 called originally Gate Helmsley, being incidentally the first to close on the branch. The confusion of having another Helmsley in the county was obvious, so that Holtby, a village lying some two miles off to the south, was chosen. There was, happily, no nonsense about Stamford Bridge which lay just to the south of the village, the low viaduct over the Derwent skirting the south side of the battlefield as companion to the medieval road bridge which closed off the north side.

A later addition to the line was Fangfoss, and then came Pocklington, a busy little town with a boys' boarding school of some local repute. So important did the Y&NM deem the place that they favoured it with an overall roof to the station, a feature which lasted until the closure and indeed beyond, as the same boys' school has purchased the premises-cum-roof for a sports hall, with some success in the adaptation.

The whole of the branch had sixteen level crossings of varying degrees of importance with, however, two or three bridges over cuttings. There were three level crossings within the Pocklington station area alone. Like Driffield and Beverley, Pocklington had its own canal which ran to the Derwent at Cottingwith. This was in poor financial shape and was given the death sentence by the Y&NM who bought it up and then left it to decay.

Before Market Weighton, three other stations must be mentioned. One was a private halt built to serve George Hudson's Londesborough residence, a large estate to the north-east of the line backed by the Wold hills and with an avenue of trees and an ornamental lake. Shipton village lay adjacent to, and south of, the line, but Shipton station nearby became Londesborough,

Brough Old Station, Hull and Selby Railway (C.T. Goode)

ebuilt ex-H&BR 0-6-0 No. 2473 on an Up goods at Cottingham South, 20 May 1933 T. Rounthwaite)

A small-wheeled ex-GCR class B9 4-6-0 arrives at Beverley on a pick-up goods. The bogie van was used to transfer parcels from station to station (T. Rounthwaite)

Ex-NER class N10 0-6-2T No. 69093 crosses Anlaby Road on a transfer freight trai about 1958 (C.T. Goode)

Class D49 No. 62750 'The Pytchley' rests beneath the roof of Beverley Station (C.T. Goode)

Small-boilered ex-GNR Atlantic on a Down Sheffield-Hull express near Ferriby (T. Rounthwaite)

Stopping train with D17 class 4-4-0 No. 1632 leaving Ferriby for Selby (T. Rounthwaite)

A Liverpool-Hull express headed by a B1 class 4-6-0 passes Gilberdyke, then (Staddlethorpe Jc. (C.T. Goode)

probably on closure of the private halt. Burnby station became Nunburnholme and thus, once more, the adjacent village gave way to the more remote village, in this instance up a small valley. The line turned east to enter Market Weighton with its all-over roof and low line of building with neat portico. Originally the station was a terminus, and had a goods shed at the eastern end and a small two-road engine shed to the north side. Here an attempt was made to bring the line into the village and close to the church and hotel.

The Y&NM line from Selby to Market Weighton was opened in August 1848, a little later than anticipated, due to problems with local landowners over the sitings of sidings and stations, among them the Vicar of Bubwith who seems to have embroiled himself in land deals and to have felt that he had a right to contest the position of the station there.

Setting aside the overall roofs, the original stations were rather mean affairs with little or no shelter out on the platforms, as awnings were not erected. Many of the stations on the Selby-Market Weighton line were of the crudest, the principal ones being at Bubwith and Holme as they both served larger villages which were within reasonable distance. West of Bubwith the line crossed the Derwent by a substantial bridge. Several of the smaller stations had 'Gate' tacked on to the end, rather in the manner of 'Road' as once practised by the GWR, both terms meaning to the initiated: 'you will have a long walk'.

First out of Selby was Cliff Common Gate, then Duffield Gate which vanished early from the scene, Menthorpe Gate and Bubwith. Between Bubwith and Holme was Foggathorpe Gate, after which came an important level crossing with the holiday road traffic for the Coast. The last station before Market Weighton was Harswell Gate, which later became Everingham after the estate to the north of it. All the stations eventually dropped the word 'Gate', except for Menthorpe Gate which retained it to the end, possibly as a form of compensation for the extremely desolate setting with only three nearby houses for company. High Field station was a later North Eastern addition, very near to Bubwith and was probably opened to keep the local incumbent sweet; he had originally wanted Bubwith station at this point. Initially the line was single and was not doubled until 1890 when the section from Market Weighton to Driffield was constructed, opening the way to holiday traffic.

Chapter 3

Along the Hull and Selby Line

The route of the original Hull and Selby Railway lies through countryside which is flat and without a great deal of interest as regards topographical or engineering features. On leaving the Selby bridge the line swings round towards the east, threading its way between the Oil and Cattle Cake Mills of B.O.C.M. to Barlby Jc. where, until the installation of the power panel in Selby West cabin at the other end of the town which controls the whole area, there was latterly a large cabin of almost 100 levers in two frames set back to back in the fork where the York and Hull lines part company. The Doncaster-Selby-York line of January 1871 is common to the Selby-Hull line through Selby, and the point of junction here was set well back from the point of divergence, Hull-bound traffic first passing from the Down to the Up Main, thus proceeding wrong line for a short way before turning off.

Once round the corner, leaving the York line to curve away sharply to the north, the Market Weighton branch took a straight route away to the north-east. This junction was also later worked from Barlby, as well as sidings to various factories on the south side of the Hull line. North of the Market Weighton branch was a clutter of mysterious looking buildings served by a siding and frame whose name gave the game away—'Powder Magazine'. A curve sited here from the east to the north could have given through running lines between Hull and York, avoiding Selby and saving a reversal there. This idea might also have obviated the need for an independent line from Beverley to York via Market Weighton; however, no such idea ever materialised.

The first station on the Hull-Selby line was Cliff, named after the straggling collection of houses by the station along one street. Eventually the station was renamed Hemingbrough after the larger village 1½ miles to the south-east, noted for its church with very tall spire. Possibly the station name was changed when Cliff Common on the Market Weighton line was opened. Station buildings at Hemingbrough were on the north side, together with the Down platform on the west side of the level crossing. The cabin and Up platform on the East side, the station being staggered. A large malthouse and goods yards were also on the north side. Hemingbrough was the first station on the Hull and Selby railway to be closed, the rest remaining open at the time of writing.

Three miles beyond Hemingbrough is Wressle station, quite near the river Derwent which is crossed by a substantial bridge. Shortly after this point the river empties into the Ouse and, due to the tidal effect, has a remarkable rise and fall and is thus well banked up on either side. Wressle village, sometimes spelt Wressell, is small and lies to the north of the station quite close by. Wressle has both its platforms to the east of the level crossing which is controlled by a cabin on the west side sited to the north. Opposite was a small goods yard. The station premises are on the south side which is furthest from the village.

At Howden, too, the next station at 2¾ miles, the buildings, of similar design to Hemingbrough and Wressle, are on the side more remote from the village. Howden village enjoyed some importance as a staging post for coaches in the old days and has many old buildings as well as the fine church, once a monastic place. It gained its importance through its situation where the road from Hull to Selby and Goole to Brighton crossed. On the Hull and Selby line Howden station lay at a good mile distant from the village, on the north side, and as no deflection was allowed to spoil the straightness of the beautiful line, so the villagers had to walk to the trains or use the horse cab which plied to and from the Station tavern. No nearer place for the station could in fact be found, and it must have been a source of great joy to the people of Howden when the princely station was opened by the Hull and Barnsley in the centre of the village much later on. At Howden the platforms were staggered, the Up platform for Selby placed west of the level crossing opposite the station buildings, with the signal box opposite the other platform.

A mile to the east the Hull and Selby was crossed by its first substantial road bridge carrying the road from Howden to Bridlington. North of the line, by the bridge a siding was put in, probably in NER days, to accommodate local traffic and controlled from Caville Bridge signal box, a small wooden structure. Bridges began to proliferate round this area, as originally another road bridge was encountered, a skew structure before Eastrington station. Between the two aforementioned bridges the H&B crossed the older line by a substantial lattice girder bridge, also on the skew. (Both companies also had competing stations at Eastrington). Eastrington station was quite close to the main A63 trunk road which crossed the line by the skew bridge, described originally as 'handsome' with a flat roof on cast iron beams supporting a number of narrow longitudinal arches of brick and stone. This was replaced by a structure somewhat unusual for a roadway, a bowstring girder bridge, at a much later date, and the interesting thing at the site is that the typical remains of the roads at either side of the line would make it appear that a level crossing had existed at that point. Not so, however, according to McTurk. Recently, a fine new roadway has been built to carry the M62 roadway across the line.

Soon after the crossing of the line by the main road Staddlethorpe station was reached, where a stationary engine was originally provided to pump water for locomotive purposes from a pond on the south side, now the resort of anglers. Here was a siding north of the line to a flax mill, while more than the usual number of sidings were to be found on the opposite side by the east end. Staddlethorpe itself was a mere hamlet, the nearest place of any size being Gilberdyke which was strung out along the main highway. Originally the local road from Gilberdyke to Blacktoft crossed the line on the level, and round the station buildings on the north side were to be found two or three houses and the local inn.

On 30th. July 1869 the line from the Goole direction was opened, which brought in traffic from the Midlands and London via Doncaster. This was to become an important link between the NER at Staddlethorpe and the South Yorkshire Railway at Thorne Jc., a vital 15 miles of line which made a route to London possible. Initially the line was born out of fear of the L&YR company who had successfully developed the port of Goole and were now looking towards establishing rail communication with Hull. Indeed, the SYR were themselves considering a similar line of route to that which was actually completed to the mutual satisfaction of all three companies with running powers all round. The two contestants were of course wise in the event, as they left the NER to pay the bill for the impressive Goole swing bridge at Skelton on the Ouse, a double-track opening swing span of 250ft. and 670 tons weight, stated at the time to be almost the largest in the world. Five run-up spans, each of 116ft. gave a total stretch of 830ft., and Goole benefited greatly from the new line, as it provided an excellent service to London which the L&Y could never equal. Spurs south of the town provided interconnection and gave the L&Y in particular a chance to escape from its dockland terminus and run via the new through station to Hull and the coast.

Staddlethorpe became well and truly extablished on the railway map and the convergence of two important routes gave signalmen working there plenty of action for many years on holiday Saturdays; in fact proposals were considered for the quadrupling of the route out of Hull and along the north bank which had become so vital. Consideration had first been given to the idea of four tracks running from Barlby Jc. at the Selby end right through to the port; in the end, however, it was decided to proceed with the work eastwards from Staddlethorpe which, along with Brough, Ferriby and Hessle was thus completely rebuilt and transformed. Staddlethorpe had light wooden platforms on each side of the slow roads only into which trains were turned as required, both Staddlethorpe West and East cabins being on the north side, the latter a wooden affair opened as required to work the yard which contained a timber yard and saw mill. The station premises were of equally light construction, resembling a cross between a green house and a cricket pavilion. The NER never did like canopies over platforms. In the fork of the junction a colony of several staff houses was provided to house the men who acted as signalmen, porters and shunters at this suddenly important place.

The short run from Goole was undistinguished except by the station at Saltmarshe about half-way along with a building in the same style as Thorne North at the southern end of the line where the NER met the MS&L. Certainly it was different from the Hull & Selby properties, with the signal box and main offices on the Up side and with a level crossing and a small yard. The attendant small village is Laxton, with Saltmarshe Hall lying one mile to the south by the river. Apparently when the line was built the Colonel Saltmarshe of the day insisted that, as he had to put up with the line crossing his land, he would have the station named after his family and be allowed to stop whatever trains he wished. There was also some restriction on Sunday services which kept down North Eastern visits to Doncaster on the Sabbath.

The Goole to Staddlethorpe line was selected for an early automatic colour light signalling system by the LNER in May 1933, eliminating a signal box at Goole station and three at the swing bridge.

The line between Staddlethorpe and Brough was quadrupled at a later period, freight trains waiting at the west of the latter station to turn in to the two road section on the heels of the passenger traffic. Water cranes were liberally provided and supplied from a triangular shaped reservoir, still visible to the north of the line by the gasworks with its two drum holders unconnected to the rail. Opposite the gasworks and to the south of the line was a corn factory, and from this point a light railway ran down to the small wharf at Brough Haven, the estuary being very close here. The station yard lay to the east of the platforms on the south side. Broomfleet station was an NER addition, primarily a goods siding with few trains until LNER days. By 1905 quadrupling of the tracks had been extended from Brough to Hessle Haven cabin, and Brough had assumed its final form with radical alterations in the form of two islands to give four platform faces, plus a new yard on the south side. The NER were very far-sighted in the layout here, as what had obviously been set out as an outer limit for a promising suburban traffic with handy run-round loops on both sides, was fully adequate after the establishment of the Blackburn Aircraft Works nearby in later years, bringing with it a vast amount of workmen's traffic each day.

The Hull & Selby railway station at Ferriby was of the humblest, with two platforms, a signal box on the south side opposite to a station building across the level crossing carrying Humber road. Beyond were Up and Down sidings on the east side. The layout was altered on quadrupling, with platforms on the slow roads carrying low wooden buildings and with a yard at the east end on the south side. With the growth of the new industries of smelting and cement manufacture by the Humber, siding connections were put in west of Ferriby at Melton Lane signal box which presided over a halt with platforms on the slow lines, which served adjacent factories at the critical times of day, including Earles Cement, which used to have one or two steam shunters.

Just outside Hessle the Hull & Selby encountered some hills reaching almost to the water's edge and enjoyed a few yards of scenery, known locally as 'Little Switzerland' where a quarry was to be found with rail access which was operationally rather awkward, as a facing connection led straight into the quarry off the Up main line only! Here too was a cutting of 40ft. depth before Hessle station was reached round a rather sharp curve. Here, the yard was to the west of the station on the south side, the platforms being opposite each other and linked by footbridge. The main station premises lay south of the station on the Up side and could only be reached rather awkwardly by Hessle folk if they first crossed the line by a bridge a fair way down. With the advent of four tracks things changed radically and for the better. A new booking office was built on the cutting top at the village side, and a walkway led down to the platform adjacent to the slow lines, where a new signal box was provided on the Up side. Due to the lie of the land Hessle was an attractive place with its canopies and footbridge, and it was most enjoyable to bask there in the sun on a station seat and see and hear the signalmen at work in the centre of the platform, bells ringing and levers rattling before a WD or something splendid on a holiday train or a fish special sped through leaving a characteristic smell in its wake. The yard at Hessle remained in the same location though augmented by coal drops, goods shed and the Company waterworks, a mysterious place with a perpetual sound about it like a droning beehive.

East of Hessle the land now became flat again, and after passing beneath the Waterside road bridge and by the shipyard, two parallel goods lines were thrown off at Hessle Haven to serve the Hull & Selby yard, leaving close to the Hessle Gas Company siding and a brickworks. The goods lines ran away independently, the passenger lines arriving at the terminus in Kingston St., a building of 100ft. by 70ft. with an entrance hall, booking office and parcels office and also ladies and gentlemen's waiting rooms. Above, reached by a 'noble staircase' were the office chambers. The train shed was 170ft. by 72ft. and was 40ft. high, the roof being raised on 22 iron columns sheltering two platforms and four lines of rail. Adjacent to the terminus was a two-storeyed warehouse and a works covering 5000 square yards for the servicing of both engines and coaches and all the appurtenances of a self-respecting railway.

When quadrupling of the main line took place, this linked up with the earlier turn-out at Hessle Haven and took away the need for a cabin for a time, though a ground frame controlled a siding to the Hessle Gas Company which had added another holder to its collection, making three. Nearby, the boatyard had come into being on the site of the brickworks.

Soon, however, the vast marshalling yards west of Hull came into being alongside the H&S run through the docks, and the newer parallel access line which swept round by a reverse curve into the Paragon Station. In 1909 the Inward and Mineral Yards were opened on the north side, with outlets controlled by Hessle Haven and Hessle East boxes. Then came a later eastern extension called Priory Yard. Needless to say, there was an Outward Yard on the Up side, used to form up the fast goods trains of beloved memory.

In December 1935 the showpiece of the area was opened, the New Inward Yard, which ran the length of the northern side of railway territory at Dairycoates. The new yard offered thirty sidings in groups of 7,8,8 and 7 respectively, with six long reception roads each with a capacity of one hundred wagons, as compared with the earlier yard with nine sidings and one reception road holding a mere 27 wagons. All inbound traffic was dealt with here, except for that from the H&B, and was sorted over the Hump for the various docks and premises. Branch line pickup traffic was dealt with here and separated into a set of six roads to await collection. The principle of the yard was the same as that found at Hamm, Banbury and March, trains being propelled over the top by special engines and the 'cuts' controlled by Fröhlich retarders and colour lights. Floodlighting enabled up to 3,000 wagons to be handled in twenty-four hours. Departures were controlled by Dairycoates West signal box.

On closure of the Outward Yard, what was left of westbound traffic was marshalled on the Down side in the Inward Yard and sent on a merry-go-round into Hull before re-appearing facing the right way. The old Hull & Selby could have arranged matters so simply with its straight line east along the river which would have taken in at a stroke, in order of their appearance, St. Andrews Dock Estension, St. Andrews Dock, William Wright and Albert Dock before reaching its own terminus at Humber Dock.

It was Albert Dock where there was always a fishing boat on the stocks for repairs, very high indeed and silhouetted against the watery background looking like a stranded whale.

The NER did a thorough, though rather messy job of linking up its sidings, yards, docks, passenger lines and engine shed on this stretch of flat land west of Hull, all made very exciting by the use of lots of signals to cover every possible move and, one suspects, quite a few impossible ones by swarms of signal arms of all sizes in slots, often on huge brackets and gantries. What the old drivers visiting the place from the more rational GC or frugal L&Y had to say on the subject might have been worth recording! These forests of brackets and gantries were a feature of the riverbank right back to Staddlethorpe, now alas almost gone. Big boxes with bay windows in the yards called Dairycoates East and West, St. Andrews Dock and a very important cabin at Hessle Road all played their part, the latter having the unenviable pleasure of funneling three routes into an Up and Down bottleneck over a main thoroughfare on the level with a tram route thrown in, fanning out to two further routes. This headache was removed in October 1962 by the provision of a new road bridge, called locally a 'flyover' for some peculiar reason.

Three level crossings nearer to Paragon and another 'flyover' replaced a further notorious headache at Anlaby Road where the traffic tended to be heavier, still with trams to control but having only one junction where the Victoria Dock took off on the city side of the crossing. This was closed in October 1964, and in May 1965 a curve was put in to allow holiday traffic for the direction of Bridlington to swing round and join the branch from Paragon, obviating the necessity of reversal there and closing the original route from Humber Dock via Hessle Road to Cottington South, the 'straight line' along which so much traffic had passed, to the puzzlement of the uninitiated who would look out and wonder how their train could pass through the city and not stop anywhere.

The 'straight line' had a 'Platform', as the GWR would have called it, at Newington near the tram depot where the line crossed the Anlaby road. This was of necessity a very narrow affair and was probably erected there for private purposes.

Chapter 4

The Route to Bridlington

'It is a matter of great congratulation, not only to the Corporation, but to every inhabitant of the town, that the undertaking which has been opened in so triumphant a manner this day, is now completed. It is one of the most complete railways that I ever travelled thirty miles over in my life. Considering the very short period of time which has been taken in the construction of this railway, I do not think it a most extraordinary circumstance that we should be in such a state of perfection this day. I could not help being struck by the fact that we should travel over such an extent of line without passing under any bridge, and the deepest cutting I saw extended only for a few yards, and was not deeper than half the height of the room in which we now stand.'

Thus spoke Mr John Gresham, Mayor of Hull, of the Hull & Bridlington Railway at its opening ceremony on 2nd. October 1846 in the Music Hall in Hull. As we have seen, the line ran up northwards from the Humber Dock terminus, past Hessle Road junction up to Cottingham, a portion of this 'straight line' remaining with its level crossings, when the link was put in to enable a run in and out of the new Paragon Station, rightly considered a more fitting and less fishy place to arrive at.

The Bridlington route took the centre of the three way junction at West Parade, leaving Botanic Gardens shed on the right, and soon crossed a right-angled flat crossing with the Victoria Dock Branch, also a piece of line left from the days of the Humber Dock. Here was a small signal box which also admitted trains of empty coaching stock to the carriage depot on the Down side adjacent to the cricket ground. On removal of these sidings, the special loop was put in during 1965, by which services which had formerly used the old 'straight line' prior to its closure could now swing round to avoid Hull. The curve is a tight one and taken very respectfully by the holiday trains. At about the same time the flat crossing of the Victoria Dock line was abolished and the short section of line to Botanic Gardens lifted. In days gone by it had been used as a triangle to turn locos. arriving in Hull which would nose up to Anlaby Road gates, there being room to do so with these closed, before running back to the station again.

At the top end of the carriage sidings was Walton Street crossing, very skew with a skew signal box on the Up side in the same style as the one at Grosmont, namely slender at the base and fully blown at the top. For many years the long gates have been operated by power. Beyond them, a spur line running up to the west brought H&B traffic to the NER after Grouping. The old H&B line crosses a little way ahead. After this bridge the route curves firmly round northwards past the Ideal Boiler Works on the Up side where a little green steam engine used to linger in its personal shed, making sorties now and then to worry the vans left behind by the pickup train.

Class K3 2-6-0 on a Down empty cattle train at Staddlethorpe; the Doncaster branch goes off to the left: 1959 (C.T. Goode)

Reboilered ex-H&B 0-6-0 leaving Driffield over the Market Weighton line with a return holiday train (T. Rounthwaite)

Ex-GNR 4-4-0 No. 4345 on a train from Leeds at Bridlington in 1930 (T. Rounthwaite)

Class D20 No. 62387 gets away from Driffield on a Hull train; note the all-over roof (T. Rounthwaite)

Cottingham South signal box controlled the sidings here, and also the point at which the 'straight line' came in, true to its nickname, from Hessle Road. Needless to say, Cottingham South Jc. was nowhere near Cottingham itself, this large village being a mile or two further north, the station heralded by a level crossing supervised by a temporary-looking cabin called Thwaite Gates. Between here and the North box, which controlled the yard on the west side was Cottingham Station, a plain affair with its single storey building, the booking office at the south end, and mammoth bicycle compounds at both ends, for this is real cycling country. Until recently the station was distinguished by a set of beautifully burnished copper lamps, a gas installation which had been put in during the sixties. At the isolated crossing called Beverley Parks that town's Minster comes into view, then the town itself and station with its four level crossings, two on either side, at Flemingate, the Station, Cherry Tree and North which takes across the road to Hornsea and Bridlington. The goods yard flanked the line beyond the station as far as the latter crossing, beyond which the Market Weighton to York line diverged to the left. This double line followed a generally rising gradient to Kipling Cotes station, set in the middle of nowhere except rolling hills and sheep famed only for an ancient local horse 'Derby', the course for this being actually served by Enthorpe on the Market Weighton to Driffield line. After closure, the station premises became 'Grannie's Attic', an antiques emporium run by the lady who managed the little tea room on the Up platform at Market Weighton, with its stained glass window proclaiming the delights to be found within. Kipling Cotes was a pleasant name. More mellifluous still was Cherry Burton, a station set between there and Beverley North, which closed before the line itself. Cherry Burton lay well outside the village, which did not realise the promise of beauty in its name.

Beverley was the terminus of the local services from Hull, which included the odd working at suitable times for the Armstrong factory adjacent to the station, as was also a leather tannery. The Up loop at Beverley ran from the North box to the station platforms and retained the original light chairs with which it was first constructed until a day in the 60s when the hot rays of the sun caused it to buckle along quite a portion of its length, after which it was quietly removed. An extension of the same line passed round the back of the station on the east side and, until quite recently, the outlet was controlled by one of the original red fishtailed swivelling boards, complete with lantern.

Striking northwards towards Arram, the Bridlington line flanks Leconfield RAF aerodrome on the left, round which it appears to curve purposely, though this is probably due to the incidence of a deep drain. Arram station is only small, its house on the east or Up platform, these being staggered at level crossing. The signal box was beyond the level crossing on the Down side, but became disused when a small panel was put into the booking office in the bay window of the house to work the signals, though not the gates which continued to need the signalman to turn out and manhandle them. Lockington, the next station, was closed in the 50s and had the distinction of being the first to close between Hull and Bridlington. In view of its remote situation it is not surprising, as there is no settlement of any size within two miles, and Lockington village lies a good distance to the west across the main road.

Within the next two miles are three crossings, the second of which was governed by Kilnwick Gate box and given a siding for the use of farmers loading and unloading merchandise. The small cabin on the Up side contained an old type of locking frame, while the Down signal, which also carried Watton's distant, survived until the early sixties and was one of the tallest NE slotted posts in the area. Both here and at Watton, the third crossing, also with a frame and siding to a fuel storage depot, a station might well have been more profitably situated than at Lockington, as two more villages, Beswick and Watton were reasonably close on the main road.

The villages of Hutton and Cranswick are both within a mile of each other to the west of the line, the latter actually spilling across the level crossing which was chosen as the site for the station and its attendant signal box. The platforms were south of the crossing while the premises, goods shed and yard were to the north on the west side, very convenient for the villagers who have always been reasonable users of trains; in fact an increase is evident due to the building of a new estate.

Eastwards the land stretches away to the North Sea, very fertile and with its becks and drains to provide the necessary irrigation. The most important of these is the river Hull which begins its journey southwards to the Humber near Driffield on the Driffield Beck. Vessels were able to navigate up the Hull as far as Driffield using a canal from a point near Hempholme. The railway line encounters the beck which it crosses just before Driffield after crossing the 50ft. contour for the first time and running into a slight cutting. After these two features it swings round to the north east to gain the correct direction for Bridlington and keep well away from the Wolds which soon rise to 300ft. quite close to the line. The curvature offers good views on either side of the train, especially in autumn when the leaves assume a delightful auburn colour. This is pheasant country too, and one often sees opulent birds playing 'chicken' if the pun might be excused, sitting tight on one of the rails until the train is almost upon them. Drivers have been known to arrive at their destination with fine feathers in the cab. The normal procedure was to run over the poultry one way and to pause to retrieve on the return. This once happened to a sheep in the dark near Arram, though the aid of two or three passengers had to be enlisted to clear the line in this much more serious affair, one of us having to announce the demise at the nearby farm house. No retrieval here, as sheep are valuable and easily missed.

Driffield station used to have an overall roof, but this was removed after the last war and apologetic awnings put up in its place. The layout of the premises is somewhat similar to that at Beverley, though the site is smaller, more cramped and almost cut off by the goods yard which came in off the curve into the forecourt on the town side. The station had a small refreshment room, one of the small touches which always give a place a little extra importance. Where the line curved away from the south, it joined a straighter run in from the south west which was the track of the one-time Malton and Driffield Junction Railway, a concern which lasted for just a year before being taken over as part of the NER on 28th October 1854. The M&DR was originally planned to run from a terminus at Wansford along a five mile stretch to Driffield. The line left little station buildings along its line at Garton, Wetwang, Sledmere & Fimber, Burdale, Wharram, North Grimston and Settrington, before descending by a spur into Malton. The main route along a branch opened at the same time, continued on towards Pilmoor. The stations were distinctive and even had the bricks used in their construction stamped 'M&DR'. Not even the NER, who loved plastering initials on everything, reached the heights of labelling its brickwork. Possibly the Wetwang farmers and others had to be deterred from purloining them for the construction of barns, etc. The line had its own 45ft. turntable to turn the branch engine at Driffield Jc., then negotiated the main road and pursued a level course for a short way before tackling the Wolds on smart gradients of 1 in 215, 196 and 136, stiffening to 87 with a summit at Wharram beyond the Burdale tunnel of 1694yd. in length. After this came a cruel drop of 1 in 60. The route was decidedly scenic and was a feature of the Sunday round trips run from Hull from time to time, even after the regular passenger service had gone. Fimber station was one of the most well known, as it was set at a busy crossroads for all to see, and nestled across two of the arms with a level crossing at each end of the platform. The two villages were a considerable distance away, Fimber being the nearer of the two, Sledmere and its Hall scarcely figuring at about 3½ miles! Very little passenger traffic would be generated here, though farmers would find their way to it with produce and livestock. The jaunty waiting shed, here still, does service as a cricket pavilion across the way. Both Garton and Wetwang were reasonably placed for their villages, while Burdale was simply a remote stopping place on a ledge at the south end of the tunnel, the nearest village being Thixendale. There were quarries in the vicinity which helped the revenue along somewhat. Wharram had a heavy chalk traffic at one time, and Settrington were also favourably positioned, while the premises at North Grimston enjoyed a site in the village at the foot of the hill and potential traffic in race horses from the local stables.

Returning to Driffield in spirit on the little branch train known as the 'Malton Dodger', we would find that the single line is joined at Driffield West Jc., which also controlled gates on the main road, by the double track line from Market Weighton and Selby which brought quite as much traffic by rail as the road did on summer Saturdays, making the West cabin a hectic place to operate in, especially as the gates were skew. The small amount of Malton passenger traffic had largely gone by closure to passengers on 3rd June 1950, and what was left hardly entered into the reckoning. The last freight ran in October 1958.

Outside holiday times the Market Weighton line was a sleepy affair, though it had lofty beginnings as an independent Company called the Scarborough & East Riding Junction Railway of 1883 which went south the hard way, from Scarborough, then proceeding south to the Mere where a connection was picked up from the York branch, after which came a steady three miles at 1 in 100 near Folkton with a tunnel 2,540yd. long at a maximum depth of 268ft., this alone probably killing the proposal; however, the route led south via Foxholes, Rudston and Kilham, all isolated villages to this day, and at a junction at Little Kendale a spur swung east to enter Driffield station by a connection at Meadow Gates, the main route running south to Kelleythorpe, then following the final alignment to Goodmanham. Eventually the line would find its way to Howden on the H&B.

The NER scotched this proposal, but permitted fourteen miles or so over the Wolds to Market Weighton, which were opened in 1890, quite late for the railway map, but filling up a handy link between Selby and Driffield by which holidaymakers from places like Idle and Cleckheaton were able to pour into Filey and Scarborough; in fact the coming of the line must have made a vast difference to the income of these resorts, though some of the traffic would have been worked round via Hull. The line was worked by the NER but remained independent until 1914. There were stations at Southburn, Bainton, Middleton-on-the-Wolds and Enthorpe, the last being little more than a block post on the line serving one country house and a field of sheep. As mentioned earlier, the station was adjacent to Kipling Cotes racecourse which was nowhere near Kipling Cotes station on the Beverley line. Middleton was situated in the village, while Bainton and Southburn lay within good walking distance. Bainton station survives almost intact as a private house whose owner, believed to be a retired schoolmaster, has sensibly kept to the spirit of the thing by retaining much of the yard area and station platforms.

The yard at Driffield covered both sides of the line at the north east end of the station, with sidings serving a sugar mill and oil and cake mill on the Up side adjacent to Wansford crossing. The outer ends of the siding outlets were extended as loops to a cabin at Meadow Gates. Stations between here and Bridlington were at Nafferton, Lowthorpe, Burton Agnes and Carnaby, the order of importance as regards revenue earning potential being the same as the geographical one. Nafferton still serves a large village and closes the south end of the main street by a level crossing and flour mill, the station premises being on the north side and platforms opposite to each other. The goods yard lingered on until 1976. Lowthorpe lay in more sylvan surroundings on a slight curve with staggered platforms, the Up one nearer to Driffield, the adjacent villages of Lowthorpe and Harpham both at a discreet distance beyond the woods, so that a traveller might have gained the impression that the place was there for the convenience of grouse only

Another short run of 2½ miles brought the train to Burton Agnes, charmingly named after the village on the main road which in turn took the name from the large house just visible from the platforms. When the owner is in residence, for the house is still in private hands, a flag flies from the roof. The name of the place, incidentally, probably means no more than 'sheep farm', the agnes being a Latin adoption, possibly by one of the earlier squires. However, the name looks well on the preserved GWR locomotive. There were parallel platforms and a small yard at Burton Agnes on the Down side, with a special siding for horse boxes on the Up. Prior to 1939 the station used to have attractive station gardens which rated highly in the competitions of the time.

The last longish run before Bridlington was to Carnaby which served its village in the same manner as Burton Agnes, though suffering more from a loss of revenue in that the bus ride on the main road to Bridlington was shorter. However, on the Up side the station was made lively in wartime by an aerodrome, for which extra sidings were laid in. The station buildings here are of different and more humble type from those at the last three places, being set at right angles to the road and on the wilder side of the line, away from the signal box which was opposite. This was a low affair with an old lever frame similar to that at Kilnwick. The fortunes of a little station such as Carnaby can be hinted at by the following returns of tickets collected at certain times which included the busy war period:

May 1926	99	(General Strike during this time.)
August 1929	202	
August 1937	332	
December 1937	77	
August 1939	205	
October 1942	102	
October 1943	10,935	(All Workmen's except 243.)
December 1946	134	(Only 5 Workmen's tickets here.)
August 1952	93	
October 1959	188	(The last time over hundred taken.)
August 1963	25	
December 1969	24	(Last complete month operational.)

The approach to the seaside when Bridlington was in its heyday was heralded by the appearance of Up and Down relief lines on the east side, all four tracks being carried beneath the only bridge on the Hull route, which replaced a level crossing, to pass the large Bridlington South cabin with 125 levers on the left and a three road engine shed with a 55ft. turntable and stabling for nine engines on the right. As if to impress after a somewhat prosaic run, the NER provided a couple of impressive gantries and another road overbridge before reaching the large station which became part through, part terminus. The original station was that portion to the west of the site adjacent to the Town Hall, with its two platforms covered by an overall roof, the west side being open-railed to a cab drive for passengers requiring vehicles or to gain the old part of the town easily which is about ten minutes' walk away on this side. To reach the seaside and the newer Bridlington which attends it, passengers crossed by a footbridge. In 1911-12 Platforms 5 and 6 were added, together with the present run of offices and pleasant covered concourse with its hanging baskets of flowers and penny-in-the-slot model of the 'Rocket'. Altogether one of the happiest of arrivals for passengers, due to staff dedication and a sensibly designed roof. At a later date Platforms 7 and 8 were constructed outside the main station to the east. These were for excursion work and had their own booking and toilet facilities which were heavily used during the season until recently. Provision of Platform 5 in particular caused a radical change in platform operation, this being devoted to Up traffic while the original Up and Down lines beneath the roof both became arrival lines from the south. The overall roof here was always very dark and was dismantled in 1962. North of Platform 1 was a secondary 42ft. turntable which also disappeared a little earlier. The original Y&NM offices were left standing on Platforms 3 and 4 and became houses.

The goods yard at Bridlington deserves comment. It was situated away from the station on the north east side across the approach road; in consequence shunting movements had to be controlled by a flagman and a separate ground frame was provided. This line was built on land alongside a branch which originally ran for a mile or so to the sea front across Hilderthorpe road on the level. The track disappeared many years ago, though its course behind Windsor Crescent is still visible.

The first Y&NM station at Bridlington was of two platforms covered by an all-over roof. The first indications of one's arrival were the coal drops on the left and a small engine shed on the right before the first of three level crossings. From extant plans the first track layout of the station is hard to fathom, this apparently based on a scissors crossover beyond the platforms. A later plan gives a more orthodox layout based on Up and Down lines together with the aforementioned Quay branch, the rails of which were in position up to around 1917.

Almost off the platform ends at Bridlington and certainly by the time the Gasworks siding was reached, the long gradient of 1 in 92 begins up past Flamborough and Bempton station to just short of Speeton. Excellent cliff and sea views are obtainable, while at times in winter snow can come in easily from the east. The author remembers calling at Flamborough station in December round about 1968. Having entered the building when the weather was calm and dry, he was astonished to find, when he emerged only twenty minutes later, that the whole area was white over to a depth of an inch or so. Flamborough station was originally called Marton, a more sensible nomenclature, as Marton Hall was by the station, whereas Flamborough and its cliffs were three miles away to the east. The station at one time dealt in a brisk crab traffic, as well as holidaymakers who now arrive with their caravans and litter up the nearby fields. Both Bempton and Speeton are small stations quite near their respective villages, the latter rather wildly situated at the point where the line passes from east to west. The route turns from west northwards following the curve of Filey bay and enters pleasant wooded country at Hunmanby, a solid little station where the signal box and waiting room have been built together end to end on the Down side. The large building away beyond the village on the landward side is a large girls' school, part boarding which has generated much traffic here in the past.

Prior to the arrival at Filey station, a layout was encountered which would have been undreamed of when the line was first opened, that is, the triangle at Royal Oak which led to the terminal spur of Butlin's Holiday Camp station, opened with ceremony on 10th May 1947. The layout consisted of two islands which provide four platform faces each, at 900ft. long enough to cater for the heavy holiday traffic which originally came from as far afield as King's Cross. A K3 2-6-0 No. 61846 carried out its own inaugural ceremony shortly after the opening by arriving at the station out of control with a rake of (fortunately) empty coaches. The spot was always expensive to operate, needing signalmen at the three corners of the triangle, though two were necessary gatemen, and the layout and station have now closed. The station was linked to the Camp by a subway under the main road, while passengers were met by Butlin's own 'Noddy' trains.

Filey Town station is the last station in the old East Riding and is well placed in the little town which has a pretty coastline to commend it and which is rather sadly underrated as a holiday resort, being overshadowed by its larger, conference-minded neighbours. The station was given an overall roof which it still has, though from the present signs the Engineer is seeking to remove it bit by bit, hoping that no one will notice. An interesting feature is the footbridge at the south end which descends outside the wall on the Down side. On the opposite platform, facing the town, are the principal buildings in more or less the same style as Beverley.

The line continues for a few miles further to meet the York-Scarborough route at Seamer Jc., with stations at Gristhorpe and Cayton Bay, closed in 1959 and 1952 respectively.

Chapter 5

Market Weighton to the Coast

Passenger traffic on the routes passing through Market Weighton comprised through traffic between Hull and York and connections beyond, and the West Riding holiday trains in the high season and a limited amount of long distance traffic between Bridlington, Selby and Leeds. Local traffic hardly entered into the reckoning at all, except for schoolchildren and the faithful few who always keep a station alive by their commuting. In the first instance, three trains each way ran from York, and two from Selby, with an odd Tuesday market service from Market Weighton at 6.30 running to Hull via Selby—how much easier did the later link via Beverley make matters! With the application of cheap day tickets this service was a success and was started back from Pocklington in 1851, giving an interesting zig-zag run. Huntington, perhaps rather strangely in view of its position, was not a very profitable station initially, such revenue often depending heavily on the 'push' of the Station Master who was expected to go out and sell whatever facilities the station had to offer.

After some opposition from Lord Hotham of Dalton Holme over land purchase, which lasted for nearly twenty years, the Beverley line was opened on 1st May 1865 with its run up to Kipling Cotes and down through Cherry Burton. The opening livened up the York-Market Weighton section considerably, and created four stopping trains each way with a Thursday-only market service from Hull. An interesting working was the midday goods from Market Weighton to Beverley which had a passenger coach in its formation, returning roughly 1½ hours later.

On the opening of the Driffield-Market Weighton section of line in 1890 which was double throughout and which also led to the doubling of the Selby-Market Weighton-Beverley sections, a strong service of 10-12 trains operated, some through to Selby and most running north of Market Weighton through to Bridlington. With the frequent unpredictability of the Victorian strange notes would appear in the tables advising passengers that a train would stop at Everingham to take up for King's Cross only, or would call at Kiplings Cotes or Cherry Burton to take up First Class passengers only, as if such a distinction mattered as the train had to stop in any case. Enthorpe was a hide and seek station, being totally invisible from the surrounding fields as the line lay in cutting. The only sign that something was afoot was a pair of railway cottages and almost nothing else around. The station had trains on only certain days of the week at first, but then became a habitual stop like other places.

There can be nothing more disconcerting to a train crew than stopping at a station where no exchange of passengers occurs, in fact they often grow to assume with habit that none will be forthcoming. The author remembers getting on the 4.32 p.m. from Bridlington at Carnaby one winter's day and

An A8 4-6-2T gets away from Beverley on a Bridlington train, July 1950 (C.T. Goode)

At Bridlington, D49 No. 62769 'The Oakley' waits to head north to Scarborough in 1950 (C.T. Goode)

Burdale in July 1969; the remains of the station are in the dark trees to the right of the extensive chalk-pits (R.W. Kidner)

Standard 2-6-0 No. 77010 shunting across the station approach at Bridlington (C.T. Goode)

being called upon by the guard who was most intrigued to know in the politest way what he was doing getting on his train there, etc, etc. The impact on the station staff is often greater. At Wressle the signalman, seeing a passenger, came down from his box, opened the little booking office and said: 'I'm going to enjoy this. We don't get many people like you!' Wressle, now unstaffed, had LNER card tickets on issue until May 1976.

Passengers of any sort would have made an impact at Menthorpe Gate, Enthorpe Foggathorpe and High Field, where the total takings for each did not exceed £40. Other places fared better, often because of military traffic in wartime, as at Holme and Fangfoss (for RAF Full Sutton). Of the smaller stations on the Market Weighton 'cross' Middleton-on-the-Wolds was the busiest at £1,600 with Southburn a poor second at £470.

Trains at Market Weighton during the Great War period reveal something of the activities on the lines in question:

DOWN LINE

From:	*arr.*	*To:*	
York Slow	7.29am	Hull	Stops at Fangfoss by request only.
York XP	7.54	Bridlington Slow	
Selby Slow	9.20	Bridlington Semi-fast	Stops Burton Agnes to set down [from Selby and beyond.
York XP	9.54	Beverley, Hull	
York XP	10.28	Beverley, Hull	
Selby Slow	10.56	Driffield Slow, then XP to Bridlington	
York Slow	12.37pm	Hull	
Selby Slow	2.07	Driffield Slow then XP to Bridlington	Thursdays only.
Selby XP	2.33	Driffield Slow then XP to Bridlington	Not Thursdays.
Selby Slow	3.18	Terminates.	Mondays only.
York Slow	3.41	Hull	
Selby XP	4.12	Bridlington Semi-fast	Sets down only at Cliff, High Field, [Holme and Everingham.
Selby Slow	5.38	Terminates.	
York Slow	5.54	Hull	
Leeds XP	6.02	Driffield Slow, then XP to Bridlington	Stops Burton Agnes to set down [from beyond Selby.
York XP	7.33	Beverley, Hull	
Selby Slow	8.25	Driffield Slow, then XP to Bridlington	
York Slow	8.59	Hull	

UP LINE

From:	*arr.*	*To:*	
Bridlington	7.35am	York XP	
Bridlington	7.42	Selby Slow	
Bridlington	8.42	Leeds XP arr. 9.45am	
Hull	8.51	Pocklington, Stamford Bdge., York	
Bridlington	10.15	Selby Slow	
Hull	10.43	York Slow	
Hull	12.47pm	York	Stops if required to set down 1st Class passengers from [Beverley or beyond and to take up 1st Class [passengers for York and beyond.
Bridlington	1.41	Selby Slow	
Hull	2.30	York	
Bridlington	2.36	Selby Slow	
Hull	4.43	York	
Bridlington	5.25	Selby XP from Market Weighton	
Hull	5.35	Pocklington, York	Takes up at Beverley only.
Bridlington	6.02	Selby Slow	
Bridlington	8.07	Selby	Stops at any intermediate station [on a handsignal.
Hull	8.22	York	

The line suffered small but significant reductions in its services as the years passed by, and during the 1939-45 period had a simple basic service of three trains stopping everywhere between Selby and Driffield. At Holme Moor, fot instance, the departures were at 9.58 a.m., 3.05 p.m. and 6.17 for Driffield, with connections for Bridlington, and at 8.23 a.m., 4.31 p.m. and 7.53 for Selby with connections for Leeds. Holme Moor also had an odd one-class only train, probably a railcar, which started from the station at 10.12 a.m. on Mondays only, and ran to Selby, calling at all stations. Rather mysterious this, but in view of the time of week and proximity of an air base, one could well imagine transport laid on for the return of weekend comforts to their abodes!

The post-war period brought the return of through holiday trains with, in 1950, two Leeds to Bridlington expresses via Selby and a novelty in the shape of a Sunday opening for a Leeds-Bridlington at around 11 o'clock, the cabins being opened again for its return at about nine o'clock. The Market Weighton-Driffield section also passed two York-Filey Camp trains on Saturdays and a York-Bridlington, Filey and Scarborough train which did not run on Saturdays.

In the reverse direction the services were unbalanced, with fast trains from Filey Camp to York and Leeds, two Bridlington-Leeds and a Scarborough-York, with a Bridlington-Bradford for good measure. The locals were still there, with departures at regular intervals at Holme Moor at 9.48 a.m., 2.48 p.m. and 6.48 for Driffield, and a ragged set of times for Selby at 8.07 a.m., 4.46 p.m., 5.01 (SO) and 8.08. The odd train still left Holme Moor, this time at 10.05 a.m. (MO).

By September 1953 there was but one summer Saturday holiday train from Leeds via York to Filey Camp, with only one train to York returning via the Wolds route. The all-stations locals had dwindled to two only, leaving Bridlington at 7.0 a.m. and 6.50 p.m., and Selby at 9.20 a.m. and 6.10 p.m. The 5.07 p.m. from Leeds carried a through coach to Bridlington which left express on the 5.45 p.m. ex Selby. There were also two round trips from Bridlington to Market Weighton and back, out of Bridlington at 7.40 a.m. express and return from Market Weighton at 8.55 a.m., and also ex-Bridlington at 4.40 p.m. express not Saturdays, back again from Market Weighton at 5.55 p.m. with one stop at Middleton.

Traffic on the line was worked very often by venerable old ex-NER 4-4-0s of Classes D17 and 20 which had seen better days on the racing ground up to Darlington; however, they could still show a clean pair of heels on the straight and level section between Barlby Jc. and Market Weighton West if required, usually with no more than two or three of the older coaches. A smart working was the transfer of the through carriage for Bridlington from Leeds at Selby, which was punched away from the station in great style, the engine usually waiting on the adjacent Down Main line for its arrival. Later comers on the services were the Selby and Bridlington D49s, equally down-graded and often in a terrible external condition. 'Yorkshire' ran for some time in the 50s with one nameplate missing. Good runs on the Selby-Market Weighton section were in fact hampered somewhat during the last war as the Down road was used for the storage of 'crippled' wagons, creating single-line working.

As far as the Saturday holiday trains were concerned, the operating picture was quite different, with locomotives of all kinds likely to appear round the curve at Driffield Jc. after their run over the Wolds. 'Directors', D9s and the large GC 4-6-0s, little J11 0-6-0s hurriedly pressed into action by Mexborough shed and doddery GN 0-6-0s from the heights of Morley and St Dunstans. Before the last war occasional LNWR engines would appear, hot foot from Stalybridge or Longsight. This glorious pageant of motive power continued into the early 60s with the mainstay of the holiday haulage, the B16 4-6-0, getting wheezier and wheezier and grimier and grimier. Failures were, alas, common, and many were the drivers who breathed a sigh of relief when they were over the top at Enthorpe. The Midland Region despatched its holiday-makers from places like Kirkby-in-Ashfield behind innocent little 4F goods engines which put up wonderful performances with heavy loads on the long runs. Then, rather abruptly, the line which, for many years, had been the approved route to Bridlington from the Doncaster direction, suddenly closed.

There had been closures already, Holtby on the York line shutting doors to passengers in September 1939, and to goods in 1951. Nunburnholme closed in March 1951. On the Selby line all the intermediate stations closed to passengers on 20th September 1954, except Menthorpe Gate which had closed earlier on 7th December 1953. They all remained open for goods traffic until Enthorpe closed completely on 14th September 1959. The rest, except Holme Moor and Everingham, finished in January 1964, the exceptions surviving until the complete closure of the line on 2nd August 1964, holiday trains being diverted via the new curve in Hull and the Bridlington line.

The introduction of diesel units to Bridlington depot in the early 60s came too late to do anything in the way of revitalising the Selby-Driffield route—there had really been little material to work on, except perhaps at Middleton-on-the-Wolds which might have expanded, given the promise of a decent railway service. Now the station here has disappeared without trace. A unit left Bridlington at 7.35 a.m., running express to Driffield and reaching Selby at 8.33 a.m. A connection at Market Weighton gave schoolboys access to Pocklington. Their return was not, however, so easy, as the only train back was the relic of the old days, the 5.07 p.m. from Leeds which left Selby at 5.47 p.m. through to Bridlington, this not on Saturdays. The only other daily train was also a Down one, leaving Selby at 9.20 a.m. and stopping additionally at Nafferton and Burton Agnes before arrival at Bridlington. This was also an odd unbalanced working, as anyone being unwise enough to travel to, say, Burton Agnes for the day from Selby would have to return via Hull, a much more lengthy proposition.

Snow occasionally blocked the Enthorpe cutting, and in 1963 the 7.35 dmu had to run down to Beverley for a time, then reverse to gain Market Weighton and Selby. One interesting train working over the line just before closure was the splendid one of a diesel-hauled rake of horse boxes taking the curve at Driffield Jc. at about 8.00a.m. *en route* from the stables at Burton Agnes via the loading dock, to somewhere like Newbury in Berkshire.

Chapter 6

Trains to Bridlington

From the operating point of view, the line serving the coast northwards from Hull may best be taken as an entity through to Scarborough, with some shorter runs to Bridlington and commuting trips to Beverley. To consider the latter first, these were originally given a separate timetable offering about 32 trains each way daily, with five on Sundays—these including, of course. the services which called on the way through to the coast and to York. Most of these trains also served Cottingham, the only intermediate station. For much of the NER's history these runs were carried out by small tank engines, usually 0-4-4s, plus several coaches operating as push and pull sets. During the later twenties and thirties the 'Sentinel' steam railcars performed on these duties. For the more ambitious trains between Hull and Scarborough, Hull and Bridlington sheds provided a steady supply of old NER 4-4-0s before the last war, with the gradual introduction of the D49 'Hunts' and 'Shires'. From time to time the old NER 'Atlantics' would be employed in the evening of their lives just before the slaughter of many good old stagers on Nationalisation in 1948. Bridlington drivers in particular were fiercely proud of their prowess and time-keeping with the big 4-4-0s, and had often to make up time due to the late connections arriving in Hull. Of course, given a flat road between Bridlington and Hull they had every chance, and the fastest scheduled time for an Up train non-stop in the early years of the century was given to the 8.22a.m. out of Scarborough which, after calling at Filey, Hunmanby and Flamborough, left Bridlington at 9.06a.m. to reach Hull 44 minutes later. What a magnificent sight the train must have been, and what sounds as it raced through beneath the overall roof at Beverley. A further non-stop left Bridlington at 8.15a.m., reeling off the 32 miles in 45 minutes. The nearest equivalent return journey was the 5.30p.m. non-stop to Bridlington only, arriving at 6.10p.m. not on Saturdays. At 4.50p.m. a more exciting train left Hull, running non-stop to Filey, a distance of 44 miles in two minutes under the hour. This train then reached Scarborough at 6.05p.m.

As on the Selby-Driffield route, the cabins and stations were opened on Sundays to pass a train which ran out from Hull at 7.00a.m., returning from Scarborough at 5.00p.m., calling at every station. A working of this nature effectively scotched any chances a gatekeeper might have had for getting away for the day, not that they could afford to in those times, though Sunday working must have yielded a little overtime pay. Occasional trips were worked on passenger trains by the A8 4-6-2Ts with their distinctive three cylinder clankety clank and a general air of purpose.

On the line from Driffield to Malton, the 'Malton Dodger' as it was called, plied up and down basically three times daily, four times on Tuesdays, Thursdays and Saturdays. A feature of the line's traffic was the shipment of odd loads of cattle attached to passenger trains, a popular one for this being the 5.30p.m. from Malton which took away the day's effort at the market there. Vans requiring attention on the way were attached in rear, while through traffic beyond Driffield, often to Nafferton, went just behind the engine. Often the train would be delayed while a van was set aside in a station siding; the Station Master at North Grimston, Mr. Richardson, sometimes had to deal with several loads of cattle there and likened the passenger train to the pickup goods. One of the last workings of this type in the district was the 6.40p.m. from Bridlington which was diesel loco-hauled in the 60s, and used to shunt the whole train bodily into the sidings at Burton Agnes in order to deal with odd vans in the rear. This could take time, but the diesel usually recovered it by the time Hull was reached. On the M&DR the principal goods traffic was stone from the quarries at Wharram and Burdale.

Until about 1959 a delightful scenic excursion left Hull on certain Sundays, running to Driffield, where it reversed, the engine, running round the train tender-first along the route of the 'Dodger'. At Malton the engine ran round again and went over the top via Goathland to Whitby, with an A8 in the lead as extra power. On the run back from Whitby the train would often come to grief on the bank at Hawsker.

Freight on the line to Bridlington produced pick-up workings by the older J21 0-6-0s and the ubiquitous GC 04 2-8-0s, as well as, in later days Class 4 2-6-0s from Hull Dairycoates. Final steam performances on the Bridlington run were in the hands of V3 2-6-2 tank engines, with the morning pick-up job for one of the remaining B16s or, a WD 2-8-0, and last of all, one of the B1 4-6-0s which featured largely during the final years, among the performers being Nos. 61002 and 61010.

During a short period around 1962 when certain of the dmus developed faults, some trains returned to steam operation, including the morning 'flyer' from Bridlington which caused the author great consternation one morning as, being unaware of the substitution, he approached Driffield on the Down 8.20a.m. arrival there to see a great column of smoke pushing upwards over the trees and feared the worst of fires in the town. However, the column was obviously moving towards our train and proved to have beneath it a grimy V3 being pushed flat out hauling a scratch rake of coaches. Arthur Dove, the driver, said afterwards that he had never enjoyed himself so much for years, and had kept good time.

The Indian summer of steam brought in many ageing and neglected engines, often old LMS types from the West Riding. As late as 1964 they continued to come in on odd Saturdays in July and August, even the little 4F 0-6-0s with cheerful loads from Westhouses and Kirby-in-Ashfield. Shed space in Bridlington was limited, and some engines, including at this late date a rebuilt 'Royal Scot', possibly 46100 herself which was at Farnley Jc. at this time, were run back light to Driffield to be parked in the short Down siding at the south end. The corresponding Up siding at the north end had, until their withdrawal, played daily host to one of the 'Sentinel' shunters of Bridlington, which would be out-stationed there for shunting purposes.

One of the last runs with steam was a daily high season working from Doncaster to Bridlington, forming a day excursion, returning from the special platforms at 6.15p.m. A Doncaster B1 was used, and it was a memorable sight to see the crew there at the shed at 4.30p.m., trimming the coal and oiling round. With the arrival before lunch, the turn would by a coveted one at Doncaster and give the men a good day's outing.

The following table shows the impact of a busy holiday period on a normally quiet country signal box. It gives the origin and destination of all trains passing Lowthorpe heading towards the coast on August Bank Holiday Saturday, 1952. During the same period 32 trains passed in the Up direction, and for all of these level crossing gates had to be opened and closed. All would of course be steam-hauled, and the Yard pilot would be a 'Sentinel' shunter scurrying home from Driffield. Light engines would be sent to various places to act as stand-by and also to take forward unbalanced workings.

Time passing			
8.27am	Three Light Engines	11.29	Leeds-Bridlington
8.30	Hull-Scarborough	11.37	Bradford-Bridlington
8.38	Two Light Engines	11.43	York-Filey Camp
8.49	Whetstone-Scarborough	11.48	Leeds-Bridlington
8.58	Leeds-Bridlington	11.55	Stalybridge-Filey Camp
9.04	Light Engine	12.07pm	Hull-Bridlington
9.14	Light Engine	12.24	Manchester-Filey Camp
9.19	Hull-Scarborough	12.26	Leicester-Scarborough
9.26	Leeds-Bridlington	12.47	Sowerby Bdge-Bridlington
9.36	Hull-Scarborough	12.53	Silkstone-Scarborough
9.44	Market Weighton-Bridlington	12.58	Sheffield Vic.-Filey Camp
9.50	Sheffield Vic.-Bridlington	1.06	Hull-Bridlington
9.57	Yard Pilot enters yard	1.14	Worcester-Filey Camp
10.01	Rotherham-Bridlington	1.18	King's Cross-Filey Camp
10.04	Yard Pilot leaves	1.40	Liverpool-Filey Camp
10.20	Hull-Bridlington	1.45	Hull-Scarborough
10.45	Selby-Bridlington (stops)	1.55	Manchester-Filey Camp
10.48	Leeds-Bridlington	2.08	Basford-Filey Camp
10.56	Sheffield Vic.-Bridlington	2.21	York-Filey Camp
11.00	Hull-Scarborough	2.39	Hull-Scarborough (stops)
11.24	Hull-Scarborough (stops)		

Chapter 7

The Hull & Barnsley is Born

Time now to return to the early days when railways were still fresh on the scene, and to examine the ultimate monopoly of the NER, which was to cause much hard thinking among the fiercely independent merchants of Hull.

Even as early as 1845, at the height of the Railway Mania, a scheme was suggested which pre-dated the Hull & Barnsley Railway by some forty years; this being a route to link the two centres of Hull and Barnsley or, more correctly, the Hull and Selby with the South Yorkshire company and its valuable connections with Sheffield and Manchester. Hull's status as Third Port was emphasised, as was also the desirability of securing good communications with the manufacturing areas instead of the rather tortuous routes available at the time. The foreseeing eye took in not just a few cities but potentially the whole of Lancashire, Wales and the Potteries, and stress was laid on the directness of such a new line with its saving in time. Physically the line would leave the H&S at either Selby or Howden, preferably the latter place, with eventual branches to Market Weighton or Driffield, thus predating the later HB&WR Jc., and to the Midland at Swinton which would open up a good route to London.

After eighteen months of intense activity the project failed in 1847, the main reason being the machinations of George Hudson who was shrewd enough and sufficiently powerful to sense that he would lose much traffic. The Corporation of York also objected to yet another bridge hampering their river traffic which, as was clearly pointed out in the reports, had greatly diminished because of the predatory activities of the Y&NM.

So the matter was shelved and was to appear again later on. The NER became a monopoly in the Hull area and found itself in the position of having, by 1872, more traffic on its hands than it could really cope with, often taking over a week to deliver goods or to collect them. Orders for forwarding were sometimes refused, and the most sensitive of all commodities, fish, was suffering through delay. The NER was acutely aware of its shortcomings and, in 1873, allowed the MS&LR access to its own independent goods station in Kingston St. However, this was not sufficient to deter the business men of Hull from a renewed desire to have a competitive railway of their own, expecially as they felt that, in the case of timber, the NER was favouring West Hartlepool at their expense.

The scheme evolved to parry the monopoly was the Hull, South and West Junction Railway, the line of which began on the east side of the city, running round to the north rather in the manner of the later H&BR, then down to Hessle where a tunnel took the line beneath the Humber to a point near Barton. From here the line passed south to join the MS&L line with junctions at Brigg for Retford and at Appleby for Doncaster. The new line would really have been quite short at 40 miles, but would have brought London 15 miles nearer. The idea attracted a capital of £960,000; the tunnel under the Humber would be the major work, with a length of 1¾ miles. Generally, the Lincolnshire side was in favour, and the largest landowners, Lord Yarborough and Mr. Elwes, gave their approval. However, the Bill was thrown out by the House of Lords for technical reasons involving the tunnel itself, and Hull was deprived of what might have been a useful and ingenious scheme.

No doubt the NER was doing its best though the merchants of the city were not easily convinced. It was obvious to them from a study of affairs in cities such as Leeds how the presence of two or three competing railway companies affected the rates andd efficiency of the services provided. Without any direct competitor wishing to challenge the NER on their doorstep, therefore, the obvious thing to do was to create a company of their own which might, in the first instance, be a form of advertisement to the city and, secondly, which might tap the developing and financially promising coal mines in the South Yorkshire area. Likewise, the docks were run by the Hull Dock Company and it was considered that an independent, competitive would be no harm.

The clutter around the warehouses grew, and it was Lt. Col. Gerard Smith and Mr. R. Galland who evolved the idea of a new line, to be called the Hull, Barnsley and West Riding Junction Railway and Dock Company, first discussed publicly at the Royal Station Hotel (NER territory!), at which the line to the new coalfield and the new dock was strenuously opposed by the Hull Dock Co. and the NER. Nevertheless the scheme received the Royal Assent on 26th. August 1880 and there was great rejoicing and revelry in the streets of Hull.

When out of Hull proper, the line ran first up, then down the chalk ridge of the Wolds before reaching the relief of the plains for a few miles and coming to the coal bearing land between Barnsdale Bar and Cudworth. It was opened to passenger traffic on 27th. July 1885 and the Alexander Dock opened eleven days earlier. The construction was carried out speedily, though the difficult nature of the work raised the cost to £101,900 per mile, with the result that economies had to be made from the outset and what was to have been a fine terminal proposed for Kingston Square near the New Theatre was cut back to utilise the carriage sheds in Cannon Street, near St. Paul's church and off Charles Street.

The new company fared so badly in the war of rates waged by the NER and Hull Dock Co. who did some fierce undercutting, that by 1893 amalgamation was being hinted at and no dividends could be paid out to shareholders. The passenger revenue would have been a definite milestone around the necks of the supporters, since it was very small, and it was the new Dock and the supply of coal from South Yorkshire which saved the day to some extent.

There was, over the years, a sort of rapprochement between the H&B and NER, and by 1900 the two were considering building a Joint Dock, a venture which was eventually opened by King George V and named after him in

Sentinel Y1 shunter No. 68145 at Bridlington Quay Crossing in August 1955 (C.T. Goode)

Excursion trains at Hornsea in the 1950's (Hornsea Museum)

Ex-GER 2-4-0 No. 7483 on a train from Hull to York near York about 1928 (J.F. Dearden)

One of the former H&BR express engines, No. 2425, leaves Cottingham on an evening train to Bridlington (T. Rounthwaite)

Former NER 'Atlantic' No. 2164 leaves York on a Scarborough excursion on 2 July 1933 (R.W. Kidner)

Ex-H&BR 0-6-0 with domed boiler on Down excursion at Malton (T. Rounthwaite)

The 'Malton Dodger' entering Driffield; 2-4-2T No. 1581 (T. Rounthwaite)

Class B1 No. 61176 taking the curve for Hull at Cottingham South Junction on a train from York, 22 Aug. 1964 (D. Hardy)

1914, a few weeks before the Great War began. As in the case of many railways, the time just prior to the war was a period of prosperity for the H&BR. A new branch was opened to Wath at the 'country' end and some lively publicity told the world of fast trains to Sheffield which had connections for virtually everywhere.

The line was Down to Hull and Up to Cudworth, which was rather surprising in view of the importance of the port to the line. Born at the Cudworth end of things, the author always thought, along with the railwaymen who worked there, that here lay the most important portion where all the real work was done!

The main sweep of line came round from the docks in the east, running north of the city on embankment and round to the western side where the sidings at Springhead were located. Here also were the engine sheds and works on the north side. The short passenger branch from Cannon Street came northwards to join the main line at Sculcoates Jc. where there was a station just short of the intersection at Beverley Road, the wooden platforms and distinctive waiting sheds-cum-canopies set on the embankment with the tall brick building on the south side, its severity lessened somewhat by an apron of glass canopies all round it. The bulk of this building which, in its time, served some of the wealthiest families of Hull and also Mr. Stirling, the Locomotive Engineer, who lived close by, still survives at the time of writing as one of the few remaining H&B structures in the city.

As mentioned, Cannon Street was a makeshift affair constructed mainly of wood. Facing the street was a two-storey building which housed offices, and behind this was the approach drive sweeping round to a single storey wooden building which did, however, manage a wooden porte cochère in front. Entering from the roadway one would see, on the far right at right angles to the main block the refreshment room, the only one the company had, with the telegraph office in the left corner between it and the front. Left of the way in was the booking office, and to the right was a waiting room and completing the run of the building the Inspector's office, a toilet and the Station Master in the right hand corner. Facing the refreshment room across the inside concourse at right angles was a block containing, from left to right a porter's lobby, guards' office and parcels office. There were two main platforms separated from each other by two addition lines used for carriage storage. The arriving engine either had to propel its own train out again to obtain its release, or wait for a station pilot to attend to it. Each of the platforms had an outside face, that on the left being used as an optional third platform, the other for parcels traffic. The outer end of the right hand platform was recessed to take a loading dock for cattle, etc. There were quite substantial yards on either side to take rolling stock and to service the engines which were at a fair distance from the shed. The station was given an arched roof of three spans.

East of Springhead a triangle sent a line south to Neptune Street goods depot, crossing the NER at Hessle Road by a lattice girder bridge. It was on this line that British Railways built the halt which serves Boothferry Park football ground.

Shortly after leaving the area of the yards the route began to climb steadily up to Little Weighton station, up on the lower Wolds, with the building on the north side towards the small village. The buildings on the H&B were always distinctive and substantial, even opulent, and came in three basic grades, those here being of Class C, the smallest. On the way up the hill was Willerby & Kirkella, with the building set on the south side at the foot of the embankment and the platforms aloft with their ample canopies. Access was by subway to the Up side. Willerby had a small yard on the north side above the station. Little Weighton had a larger arrangement plus a goods shed on the south side west of the station where quite a brisk pickup traffic was exchanged. The H&B signals were distinctive and of course different from the odd-looking slotted type of the NER. Here they were rather reminiscent of the old Hornby 'M' series of 'O' gauge which used to accompany those peculiar stations made of tin which looked as if they were chopped in half lengthways. There were very tall signals at Little Weighton, both the Up and Down homes being unforgettable. Beyond the station lay Drewton tunnel of 1 mile 356 yd. into which the line fell on a generally straight course, passing through two more short bores called Sugar Loaf and Weedley before entering South Cave station at 14 miles from Cannon Street. To cope with the intensive coal traffic three extra cabins were put 'into Block' at Drewton East & West and Weedley, the first of which was burnt down in May 1929, the third being happily situated in isolated rustic surroundings.

'I remember one terrible night at Weedley box the first winter I was there. Snow fell heavily all night accompanied by a fierce north wind, the snow coming tumbling down the hillsides onto the line. I was very much afraid that some of the trains would leave the rails or be stuck. I reported the matter to the South Cave Station Master who told me to carry on as there was nothing we could do until anything happened. The trains did keep getting through, the engines being able to keep the lines clear. Mr. Bailey, the Chief Engineer, a very genial person, frequently visited Weedley and always called at the box to borrow a mug. Then he would go down to the spring close by and have a good drink of the excellent water' (recalled Mr. A. Howden *et. seq.*).

South Cave station lay a mile north of the village and was earmarked as a special site, being provided with one of the two Class 'A' buildings of some size and with provision for a refreshment room extension, if needed. The awnings, too, were superior and the Hull side platform was designed to accommodate an extra face for a loop line, which was never implemented. The yard, on the village side, was even larger than at the other two stations and did a good trade in timber and coal. Water cranes were available for thirsty engines and were supplied by a tank and a purifier on the east side of the road bridge. Almost at the foot of the gradient came North Cave, a short distance further on, with the main building set on the foot of the embankment and of similar design to Willerby. Both building and yard were on the village side which was quite close. The signal box was on the opposite side at the western end and, to the end, retained its original H&B equipment and framed track diagram. The true point where the line reached ground level was at Sandholme where the signal box controlled a level crossing of some width across the shunting necks and running lines, for here were quite sizeable yards on each side where the coal was brought by smaller engines for making up into handy loads to be taken over the hill by the larger ones. Here also was a turntable and a third running line passing behind the Hull platform which was, however, fenced off from it. A small gate box to the west, Ings Wood, turned trains in to this line as required. Possibly it was thought that Sandholme had a rosy future, as Class 'C' buildings were provided with the handsome awnings, facing towards the distant A63 road where was to be found the ribbon development of Gilberdyke. Sandholme was a complete nonentity of half a dozen houses which lay north of the line and which was exceeded in size by the railway cottages nearby. Today the station building stands derelict, looking as if waiting for the demolition man, though having been spared to survey the roaring M62 motorway which passes close by. This rather fine road has taken over part of the track bed between here and North Cave, swallowing up the intermediate station of Newport (Wallingfen in LNER days) on its high embankment by the Market Weighton canal, seemingly all wood and corrugated iron until one looked down to the north and saw the large square building set at right angles to the railway. This was a unique arrangement, the platforms being linked by wandering arcades and steps in a fascinating manner. Alas, the building, which was very beautifully kept in private hands, and the station which had won prizes in the garden competitions, simply vanished beneath the M62.

'The section of line from North Cave to Newport was on a high embankment, a section employing many builders and labourers who had their houses at Newport, or River Brigg as they knew it. It was a small inland port with its own fleet of keels and barges doing most of the transporting of coal, stone bricks, drain pipes and corn to different parts of the country as far afield as King's Lynn. When the H&B took over, many of the navvies stayed there because the place was different from most others, having neither squire nor parson living there. There were five pubs, and five religious bodies. One of their chief officials engaged in the construction of the line, Mr. Stannard, lived at The Grange, Newport. Here also were kept horses used in the construction. Several men who helped to build the line stayed on as station masters, porters and linemen. From Newport the most popular were the Hull Market ones on Tuesdays and Fridays and the Excursion to Hull on Saturdays, first train 1/8d, second a shilling, the latter returning at 11p.m.'.

'There was a serious accident at Sandholme in 1900 but no serious injuries. It was dark and around 11p.m. A Down train had stopped to detach a truck loaded with barrels of ale. To do this, the Up main had to be crossed. The truck was detached and loosely propelled across the Up line and in due course the guard, thinking that the truck had gone into the goods yard, gave the signalman permission to close the points, backed the engine on to the train and left for Hull. Unfortunately the ale had not gone into the yard but was actually standing foul of the Up main line. Shortly afterwards an Up Excursion train arrived and collided at full speed with the truck which was carried about 200 yards to the platform. Several passengers suffered minor cuts and shock, but nobody was seriously hurt. I was called out of bed to institute single line working and remained on duty until 4p.m. the next day.'

The H&B ran north of the former Hull and Selby line which, as first-comer, had the easier route along the Humber shore. West of Sandholme, however, the gap narrowed until the point west of Eastrington village where the two lines crossed, the H&B taking the southerly position and running right through Howden village, the station flanked by two road bridges, one conveying the main coast route from South Yorks., and a rather nasty skew level crossing at the west end where the A63 crossed. Howden enjoyed fame with its coaching inns at an important crossroads years before the coming of the railways, while the founding of an airship base in the thirties brought an unfulfilled promise of lasting fame. Now the place remains peaceful, its only claim to distinction being the partially ruined Priory church which forms a landmark over the level countryside.

The H&B had a future in mind for Howden and gave it the other Class 'A' building facing the village. This was similar to that at South Cave, with the peculiarity that the side which faces the platform at Cave faces outwards at Howden, the awnings being however fitted *comme il faut*. This could well have been a fault of the builder's who got his plans the wrong way round at foundation level.

There were two cabins at Howden, East and West, the former spending most of its life closed, as the West box could run round local trains as well as wrestle with the big level crossing gates in high winds. A goods shed and an active yard completed the picture. Twenty years after closure to through traffic the station here was almost beautiful with the neatest of platforms and not a weed in sight. The awnings and wooden buildings were always well painted.

'I started as Porter at Howden station in 1913. My turns of duty were from 9a.m. to 9p.m. and my wages were 20/- a week for the first year, then a rise of 1/- plus uniform which in those days was green corduroy with brass buttons and a large number on the waistcoat—mine was 61. We always had to be clean and tidy, and obliging to travellers.'

As noted earlier, the NER lay at a disadvantage a mile out of the village on the north side. Eastrington village, where the two competing lines crossed, lay between them and was also served by a station on each, both close to the village. The H&B premises were Class 'C' buildings and the interesting thing here is that the LNER selected the station to be down-graded into a halt, probably under the control of the Howden station master. However, there were two signal boxes to work the level crossings at each end, the easterly one which became known in LNER days as North Eastrington East, just to confuse, succumbing to closure in August 1928.

West of Howden the line ran due west to cross the Ouse at Drax by means of a fine swing bridge of open lattice construction. On each side of the swinging span which gave two openings to the river of 100ft. were fixed run-up spans, each of 77ft. After lying derelict for several years, the bridge was put out to tender for removal in the summer of 1976.

Beyond this point the line proceeded to Cudworth via Carlton and Kirk Smeaton, places outside the premise of this particular work. The last station before crossing the river took place served the isolated village of Barmby-on-the-Marsh which had one road only running in and out of it. Apart from the swing bridge which was serviced once a week by a BR boatman and left open to river traffic continuously, the little church with its Regency tower was worth a visit. Of the station, which lay outside the village to the east down a short lane, there is now no trace. It was erected some time after the others, in 1893, and a standard station master's house was constructed to serve as the main premises on the north side, where there was also a small goods yard.

Between Howden and Barmby lay the largish village of Asselby, where it was hoped to provide a station since the line passed close by. However, nothing came of the idea and the name was perpetuated only in the signal box which controlled a skew level crossing.

On 8th. April 1929 the LNER opened a halt at Springhead, short of Willerby station, to serve the village of Anlaby and a colony of railway houses near the embankment. The halt was too far from the shed and works to be of any real use there.

Departures from Little Weighton (see opposite)

From Hull:		*To Hull:*		
6.21am	Howden	8.24am	from	Howden
7.20	Cudworth	9.25	"	Sheffield
10.00	Sheffield	11.20	"	Cudworth
11.20	Knottingley	1.10pm	"	Cudworth
12.50pm	Sheffield	2.39	"	Sandholme (Th SO)
1.46	Sandholme (Th SO)	3.51	"	Sheffield (SO)
3.20	Sheffield	4.58	"	Carlton
4.25	North Cave	5.48	"	Cudworth
5.19	Sheffield	6.43	"	North Cave
6.07	North Cave	8.57	"	Sheffield
7.21	Cudworth	9.59	"	Sheffield
9.22	North Cave	10.13	"	North Cave

There are four trains each way on Sundays, two between Hull and Cudworth.

Chapter 8

Up to Cudworth

Less than a full page of Bradshaw gave the H&B passenger services in 1899, which was a typical year from the early period in its history. There were eight trains from Cannon Street to Cudworth which called at virtually all the stations *en route*, except for the 9.25 a.m. which omitted six and the 11.40a.m. which after Beverley Road, an obligatory stop for all trains, stopped at Howden only on the East Riding side of the Ouse. The 10.40p.m. was the best runner of the day, getting to Cudworth at 12.09a.m. after five stops. A connection brought the traveller to Sheffield Mid. by 12.52a.m. Two other slow trains left Cannon Street for Knottingley via Carlton, and there were two trains at 5.35p.m. and 9.0p.m. for North Cave only. Seven through trains operated from Cudworth in the reverse direction, the best of the day being the 5.5a.m. which took in a stop at Howden and ran in at 6.25a.m., a hearty performance for a little 2-4-0 tender engine, for these were the largest passenger locomotives of the time. The 5.5a.m. also ran on Sundays and was matched by the Up 10.20a.m. from Hull which had more stops.

On 3rd. October 1905 the H&B began through running over the MR to Sheffield, taking initially 1¾ hours with three trains each way by 1910, made up of new corridor stock and utilising the Kitson domeless 4-4-0 locos. of Class J, Nos. 33, 35, 38, 41 and 42. Speed was not their strong point, however, as they tended to linger at stations on the way. The Hull departures were at 9.40a.m., 3.0p.m. and 5.0p.m., arriving in Sheffield at 11.45a.m., 5.3p.m. and 6.55p.m. respectively. The fastest train at this time continued to be the old 5.5a.m., now the 5.10a.m. which reached Hull at 6.30a.m., still running on Sundays also. The train continued to run for several years and gained mention in 'Whitaker's Almanac' as one of the World's Fastest Trains for its performance on the flat between Carlton and Howden. An idea of the service offered in 1910 will be gained from a list of departures from Little Weighton where all but the 5.5a.m. stopped. *(See table opposite.)*

The Sheffield expresses did not survive the rigours of the Great War and went in 1917, the through service to Knottingley having vanished much earlier in March 1912 due to a haggle with the L&Y over the use of their gloomy Knottingley station, and to the Coal Strike of that year.

The number of passengers was never very great, and record has been made elsewhere of trains of three bogies arriving at Cannon Street without a single passenger on board. However, the Company's *esprit de corps* was very high and, public or no public, the staff really enjoyed playing with their huge train set and loved every minute of it. One such was George Gamwell, the Lineman at Howden for many years, who went to work at 6 a.m. on Sundays voluntarily without any renumeration 'to please himself.' In any case the goods traffic kept everyone busy, with coal, meat and butter galore. In 1897 nine express goods trains left the docks for Cudworth daily on weekdays, as well as three fast fish and two butter trains. Most of these were the really exciting trains for speed as they did not stop except, perhaps, for water and often reeled off the fifty miles under the two hours, such as the 1 p.m. fish which reached Cudworth at 2.50 p.m. The 1.30 a.m. express goods from Alexandra Dock called at Eastrington to attach vegetable traffic for London, a daily manoeuvre which must have made the platform staff's day (or rather, night).

The 'Tiny' 0-8-0 tender engines of 1907, Nos. 117-131, came to relieve the hard-pressed 0-6-0s and to take over the heavier work, which had been taxing the smaller engines and maintenance staff. At this time there were about ninety trains daily, of which half were coal. For operating purposes the line was divided at Sandholme and Springbank West, the section of hump between the two places requiring care in the loading of engines so that the smaller goods 0-6-0s of Class D, for instance, could bring up coal from South Yorkshire to Sandholme yard in loads of 38 wagons, but then either had to reduce the number to 26 for the climb to Drewton tunnel, or hand over to a 'tiny' which could cope with 40 wagons 'over the top'. These large engines could also take 65 empty wagons anywhere on the system with ease. In practice the returning wagons were unusually utilised to take pit props to the collieries, a common sight until not so long ago.

The H&B had various tank engines in Class G which were used for dock trips and for some of the local passenger workings out to Howden. The pick-up goods work at the intermediate stations was worked by the older 0-6-0s, Nos. 19A and 24A of 1885 being used for some years. The policy was to send a pick-up out from each end of the system, these meeting in the yard at Howden where, after a breather, the loads would be taken forward along with the brake van as the engine and crew exchanged them and returned to their home shed. All considered, this was a pleasant day out with some nifty work at times when a van or wagonload had to be 'kicked' across into the yard, blocking both directions in the process. Often the signalman had to decide whether to chance it or to put the whole train across before some heavy coal train came pounding through on its heels. The writer well remembers some well-chosen words at Drax when the signalman there was a little tardy at getting the pick-up organised. There were also the large cans of water and oil which had to be dropped off at the gate houses en route, each of which necessitated a halt on the running line.

Beverley Road station was fairly well placed for the monied and the influential of Hull, being on the tram route which was just a good pace or two away down Fitzroy Street. It also acted as a ticket collecting station for Cannon Street, and to the north of the site was Rodney Street where lived the important Inspectors of Signals, Traffic and Goods. Mr Stirling lived across the way in a big house facing Pearson Park and he would make use of a special engine and brake composite coach plus his own guard, Tom Carey, to take him to the works and back.

With everything to gain from advertising, the H&B did its very best in that direction, and the timetable made it quite clear that their line was in touch with everywhere of importance, usually via the Midland system. There were

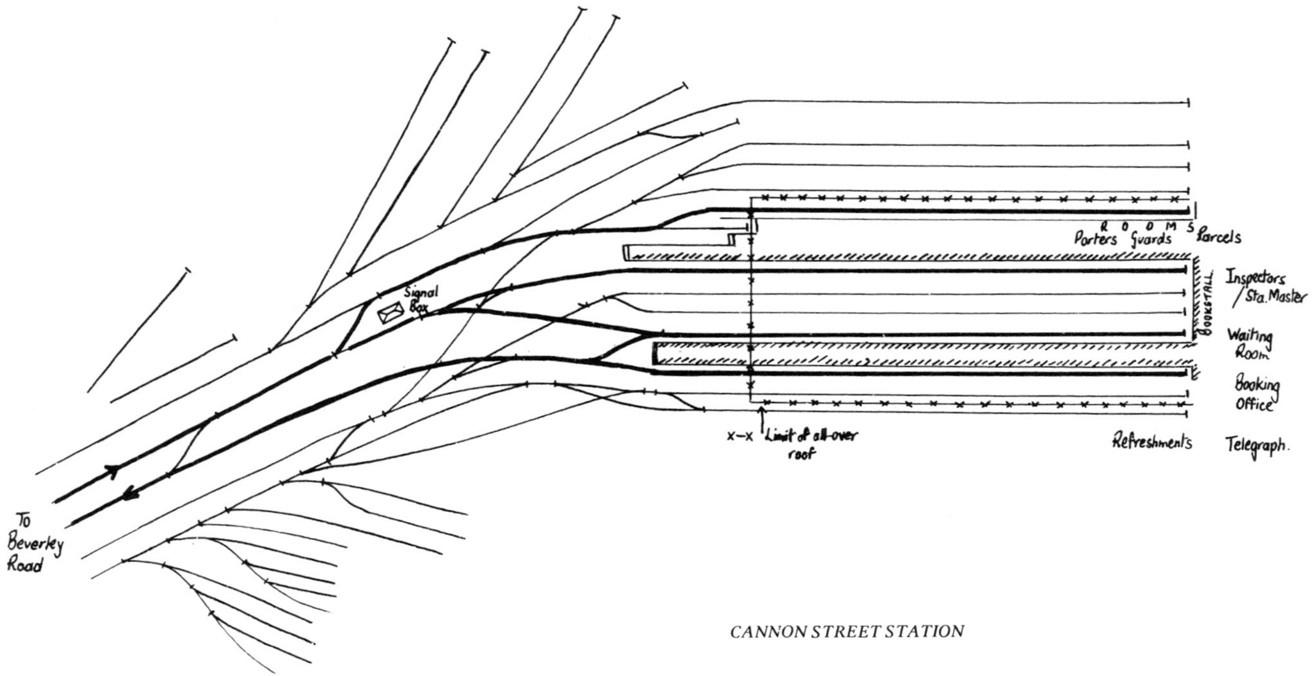

CANNON STREET STATION

An ex-LMS 'Crab'-2-6-0 brings a Midland holiday excursion through Driffield, Summer 1955 (C.T.Goode)

Up 'Yorkshire Pullman' passing Thorne Junction hauled by V1 2-6-2T No. 67635 (P. Cookson)

Much activity at Botanic Gardens station (T. Rounthwaite)

The Hull & Barnsley Railway's heavy goods engine; 0-8-0 No. 121 (Loco. Pub. Co.)

cheap tickets offered for everyone, including anglers who had to produce their rod and line at the Ticket Office (Hull to North Cave return 1/8d). An itinerant musician with harp could carry this fearsome instrument free if it weighed less than one hundredweight. Special fares which were popular were Market Returns, trips to Leeds for 2/- return, and wonderful outings on Sundays for just sixpence! Cannon Street retained seven guards for working the Sheffield expresses.

With the various categories of rates which the H&B had in mind, the story is worth setting down of the occasion at Pickburn, on one of the branches worked by the company in South Yorkshire, when a client arrived there with a coffin plus corpse for shipment to Hull. The station master was absent and, after a delay, the porter in charge weighed the item and arranged for despatch. Nothing more was said about the affair until about two or three weeks later when the station master was tidying up his ledgers and suddenly realised that his company had in fact no rate by which to charge for a coffin and corpse. On asking his porter how he had arrived at the rate to charge, which had in fact been accepted by HQ in Hull, the man stated that he had used the scale of charges applicable to animals in carcase form!

Willerby and North Cave would in fact be the busiest stations for the shorter distance services, the latter turning trains round and having a certain amount of schoolchildren to deal with. Sadly, apart from perhaps Howden which became South Howden in LNER days, none of the places was in a position to generate much passenger traffic and each lived its unhurried life until the passenger service ceased.

After the Great War it was obvious that the H&B would have to meet up with the NER sooner or later, for had it not already committed itself in the matter of the Joint Dock of 1914? In July 1922 nine trains ran each way, four serving Howden, four serving North Cave and two all the way to and from Cudworth. The Sunday flyer had gone, leaving one slow service each way on that day.

In 1922 the NER, much to the genuine grief of the H&B, took over all their assets and, it is said, immediately transferred the best Springhead craftsmen to Darlington, beginning the great run-down. To the NER passed 181 engines, and these were quickly depleted within weeks by the withdrawal of fifty, leaving only a small batch to go to the LNER. The proud 4-4-0s were given a green mantle to replace the famous 'invisible green' (which looked decidedly black) and on the tenders appeared strange numbers which just did not look right. In 1924 a spur was built down from Springbank Jc. to the NER Hull-Bridlington line at Walton St., thus enabling Cannon Street to be closed to passenger traffic as from 13th July 1924, though of course the main line remained open for goods. Beverley Road closed as well at this time, presumably losing its awnings at an early date.

When Grouping came in 1923 and the LNER was formed, the two former enemies found themselves beneath the same umbrella. The H&B trains ran as before with roughly the same mixture as in 1922. Newport station now became Wallingfen to avoid confusion with other Newports, while Carlton added 'Towers' and 'North' and 'South' came to Eastrington and Howden respectively. During the General Strike there was only one train each day between Hull and South Howden. The next significant stage in the history of the line was the introduction of a 'Sentinel' steam railcar on trial on 12th March 1928 which was to mark the start of a fairly long and reasonably happy relationship with these friendly looking (and sounding) creations.

The cars were now put into operation from 8th April 1929 on an improved service to South Howden and North Cave in an attempt to gain traffic, departures being at five minutes to most hours of the day, with an interesting short run out to Willerby and back at 1.55 p.m., all cars calling at the then new Springhead Halt. The main line workings to Cudworth were, however, allowed to slip and there were now only two trains each way daily and one on Sundays. The railcars however ran on Sunday afternoons to North Cave.

At the beginning of 1932 passenger trains west of Howden ceased, the line being used only for occasional excursions to Hull Fair or the seaside.

The H&B engines were withdrawn in great haste, the 'Tinies' all going by the end of 1931, though their boilers survived on NER 0-8-0s as rebuilt. The 4-4-0s suffered the indignity of domes and LNER numbers, these being 2425-2429, but apart from the odd runs to Bridlington and Sheffield Victoria, kept largely to the old line until withdrawal in 1934. Thirteen of the tank engines, however, kept running until after the 1939-45 hostilities and gained numbers under the LNER renumbering scheme.

Up to and during the last war the steady volume of freight on the H&BR was hauled by NER Q6 and former GCR Q4 0-8-0, as well as GCR 2-8-0s which, it must be admitted, did the work without any fuss. Coal was now being worked to Springhead and not to Alexandra Dock. Pick-up duties went to the older NER 0-6-0s and occasionally to one of the Class A tanks due for the scrapyard. Tanks of this type would appear as well as the GCR A5s which Hull had acquired on the passenger trains as the 'Sentinels' were scrapped. The tanks were not push-and-pull fitted and had to run round their coaches; the G5 0-4-4Ts which also operated on the line were able to propel their coaches and were generally satisfactory. The 4-4-2Ts of the old GNR, Class C12, also put in an appearance from time to time.

The winter of 1947 blocked the deep Drewton cutting with snow and held a train on the Down line for a month.

On 17th July 1953 diesel units were tested between Hull and South Howden, more it is suspected because the line was handy for the purpose than because of a desire to stimulate the flagging passenger service, which was now in a moribund state. Departures from Hull were as follows at this time:

6.20am	South Howden	4.30	South Howden
8.21	North Cave	5.22	South Howden
11.45 SO	South Howden	5.55	South Howden
12.20pm SX	North Cave	8.30	South Howden
1.50 SO	South Howden	10.30 SO	South Howden

These ran on weekdays only with an equivalent number of return trips. One interesting relic survived, namely that of leaving the last train stabled at Howden overnight to form the early morning departure, the engine returning light to Hull and running out each morning. On 30th July 1955 G5 No. 67337 took the 8.30 p.m. out as the last passenger train. The route through to Cudworth survived until 29th November 1958, when WD 2-8-0 No. 90352 brought the last through coal load into Springhead. The WDs had managed the mineral workings exclusively during the final years, and had performed excellently.

After a slow process of whittling down the pick-up goods, firstly by closing the line beyond Little Weighton from 6th April 1959, the whole section west of Locomotive Jc. and Springhead finished on 4th July 1964.

Thus a line vanished which at one time required extra signal cabins open between Springhead and Sandholme to create block sections for the volume of traffic, such as the 112 trains which passed through Willerby on the morning shift on a memorable Monday in 1913! The one great advantage which the H&B possessed was that it ran directly from point to point free of any major cross traffic to impede it such as the NER met with at Doncaster and Selby. Thus it could provide a service which it would be hard to match for speed nowadays considering the obstacles a train coming from Sheffield to Hull has to face today, in spite of rationalisation of the layout at Doncaster.

Its prime disadvantage lay in the terrain which severely limited the loading of its trains, and as far back as 1923 a proposal was made to drop H&B traffic down by a spur at Eastrington to the Hull-Selby line where the routes crossed, so cutting out the difficult and most interesting section. The idea was, in fact, a good one which was actually taken off the shelf and given an airing in 1963, though again without success. Had it been implemented, an alternative river crossing would have been available in the nearby Drax swing bridge, and the line, laid on the formation which still survives, would link up with the section of the line retained to serve Drax power station and which runs through Carlton station round to the L&Y line at Hensall, giving a route to Wakefield and beyond.

The remaining H&B coal traffic was transferred to the NER line or to Immingham, thus leaving no justification for the continued existence of the route. Rather pathetic and touching was the pilgrimage of WD 2-8-0 No. 90009 which, like others, found its way over the weed-ridden track to Carlton Towers on a sunny day in the spring of 1958 with nothing else for company but a brake van—a Southern one of all things—to wait for a while and then return, still with only the single vehicle.

Surviving today are various station buildings, the best being perhaps at South Cave, and the old section of main line from Springbank to Alexandra Dock plus the old Neptune St. line which is now part of the upgraded high level route from Hessle Road, free, as planned, of the curse of level crossings.

Chapter 9

Traffic Along the Humber Bank

The obvious place to start is Hull Paragon station itself. The effective station yard area began at West Parade signal box, where the three major routes joined company for the final run home, that is, the old H&S route extended from Hessle East, by the branch from Bridlington and beyond, and the Victoria Dock branch coming in from the north past Botanic Gardens shed whose outlet also connected at West Parade, bringing in traffic from the Hornsea and Withernsea directions. From West Parade six tracks fed in to the station, first negotiating a nasty level crossing just outside at Park Street which was replaced by a rather inadequate bridge. The cabins at West Parade, Park Street and Paragon were part of an old Westinghouse power signalling scheme of 1904, mustering a total of 442 levers, no mean number to operate. The signal gantries at the approaches to the station were a sight to behold.

The original Paragon station was designed by G.T. Andrews and covered 2½ acres. The main building was pillared and imposing, and still stands on the south side, being used as a parcels office. In December 1904 an enlarged station was presented to the public, with extra platforms outside the overall roof to the south, and a new booking office round the corner overlooking Paragon Square nest to the fine Royal Station Hotel. What was really an unpretentious frontage—apart from the hotel—was now concealed behind an iron canopy on stilts to cover the cabs, topped by a clock at the southern end. Hitler did his best in 1941, but only succeeded in destroying some offices and a railway museum on the site. The canopy survived until British Railways removed it in 1962 to make way for one of those modern and impersonal blocks to house the District Headquarters. Economies were made and the premises are now let out to private concerns. From the front there is little evidence that a railway station lurks behind, as any advertising is totally absent. However, a seeker after trains will soon come upon the splendid peninsular Booking Office with its many windows and 'NER' written into the tesselation to walk upon. The booking office here, being closed in, is the sort that used to make certain sadistic clerks play tricks on unsuspecting old ladies. The author did it once or twice when on holiday relief at Nottingham Midland where the same design was to be found. Old lady appears at Window 1, wanting ticket to Derby, totally unaware that there is only one open counter running the whole length of the windows inside. She is asked to go to Window 2, to be met by the same clerk who has moved down. After about the third move the game is up and a ticket is sold.

Through the Booking Hall the station proper could be reached beneath its roof of five spans covering the nine main platforms, the longest being nearly 800ft. The total number of platforms was fourteen, the extras lying outside the main roof and comprising No. 10 which was a recessed part of

9 and suitable for short trains, railcars and the like, as were Nos. 11 and 12 which often did duty as goods platforms. Nos. 13 and 14 were, however, long excursion platforms for extra and relief services. The plan will give an idea of the use to which the various offices and cubby holes round the station were put in the years before the last war. In the fifties the gents' hairdressers at the head of Platform 9 had a sudden surprise visit from a steam loco, which overshot the buffers and pushed through into the interior of the structure, giving the customers a close shave, it might be said. At about the same time the two surface level wooden gents' conveniences were replaced by a more modern subterranean facility adjacent to Platforms 5 and 6, while in recent times the normal access to the station has been via the barrier controlling these platforms, to save staff work. Other interesting alterations here have been the transformation of the old left luggage office into the larger of two refreshments buffets and, on the railway side of the barrier, the cutting back of Platforms 1 and 2 to a point well outside the roof, leaving a generous space for parking. Removal of much of the siding area on the north side has also yielded extra parking space available for road vehicles. A less fortunate step was the removal of the outer umbrella roofs over the platforms.

The nature of the traffic may best be hinted at from the use to which the twelve Booking Office windows set in carved oak panelling with accompanying cream and brown tiling with green waistband were put before some on the north side fell out of use.

1. Goole and intermediate stations. H&B stations.
2. Thorne, Doncaster, Sheffield.
3. Selby, Leeds, York.
4. Short journeys to Hessle, etc.
5. Hornsea and Withernsea.
6. Thousand mile tickets.
7. Advance bookings.
8. General.
9. Enquiries after hours.
10. York via Market Weighton.
11. Bridlington, Scarborough.
12. Seasons, Party Bookings.

Windows 1-4 were on the south side, 6-7 facing the street, 5 and 8 on the angles and 9-12 on the north side. In 1929 over one million passengers were booked in the year and, no doubt, a similar number arrived on tickets booked elsewhere. At the same period the number of trains departing was 170 daily, plus many extras on Saturdays and at holiday periods. The number of platforms was fourteen, the longest being almost 800ft. The H&B services usually left off No. 1 Platform, while the principal London trains used No. 9. Nos. 13 and 14 outside the main premises were used for excursion work.

A considerable amount of fish was received, surprisingly enough, as well as despatched in odd van loads on passenger trains, as well as fruit, milk and inward rabbit traffic. Odd vans of this nature attached to a passenger train always made an interesting sight and sound as well, and normal policy was to attach loads going all the way behind the engine and roadside deposits in the rear. Such sights are now rare, though the dmus still sometimes arrive at Hull from Doncaster with a four or six-wheeler in tow. The route to King's Cross via the branch from Staddlethorpe to Goole must be regarded as the

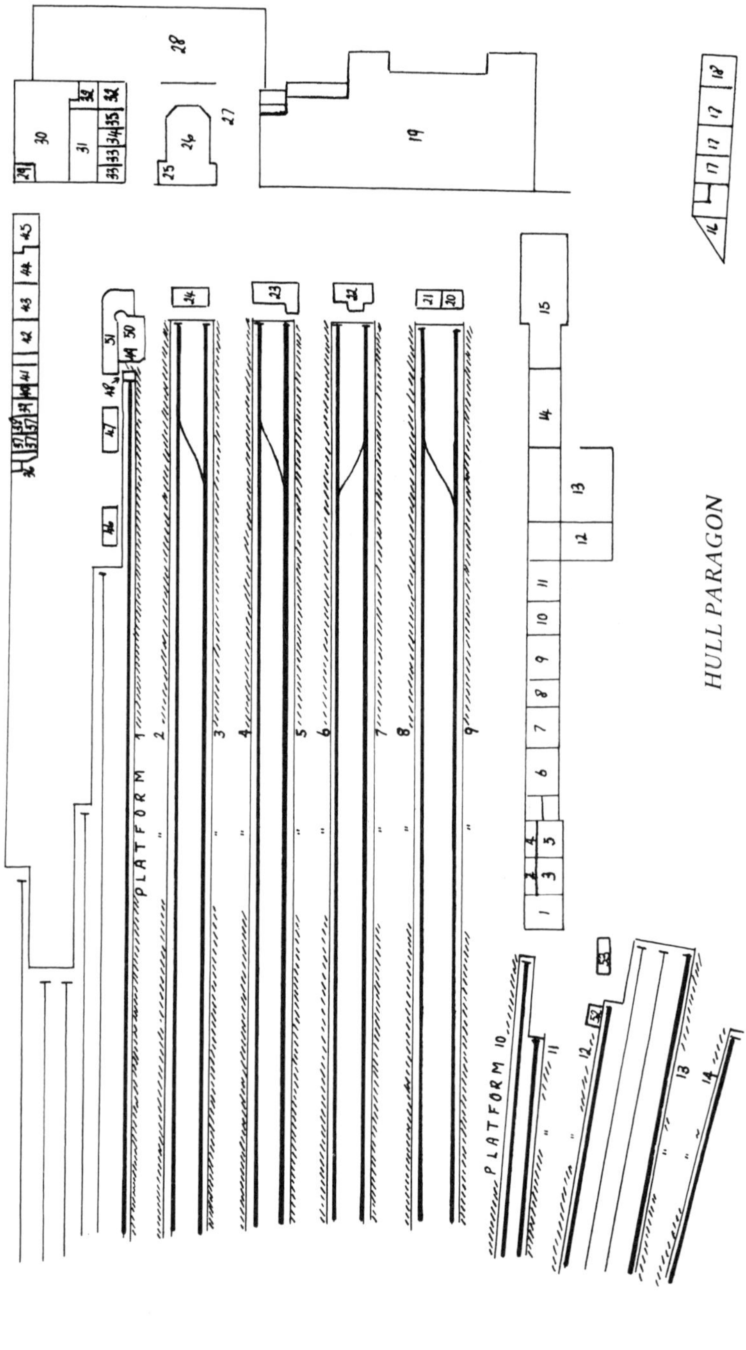

HULL PARAGON

Disposal of Offices at Hull Paragon Station before 1939

Key to the numbered plan, which is not to scale

1. Fish and Game store.
2. Oil store.
3. Lamp Room.
4. Coal store.
5. Foot warmers.
6. Guard's Room.
7. Gentlemen's Room.
8. Clerk's Lavatory.
9. General Room.
10. Ladies' Lavatory.
11. Ladies' Room.
12. Classroom.
13. Examination Room.
14. Abstract Office.
15. Parcels Office.
16. Yard.
17. Stock Room.
18. Garage.
19. Station Hotel.
20. Hairdressing (Gents.)
21. Gentlemen's Lavatory.
22. Temperance Room.
23. Refreshment Room.
24. Gentlemen's Lavatory.
25. Excess Luggage.
26. Booking Office.
27. Booking Hall.
28. Covered way for taxis.
29. Lost Luggage.
30. Left Luggage.
31. Telegraph Office.
32. Station Master's Clerks.
33. Continental Agent.
34. Assistant Station Master.
35. Station Master.
36. W.Cs.
37. Coal store.
38. Foot warmers.
39. Guards' Room.
40. Ladies' Lavatory.
41. District Engineer.
42. General Room.
43. Porters.
44. Emigrants' Luggage.
45. Foreman Porter.
46. Fish Office.
47. Milk Platform.
48. Ticket Collectors.
49. Lavatories.
50. Ladies' Room.
51. Tea Room.
52. Fish and Fruit Office.
53. Fish Stage.

principal one which, in the early years of the century, brought in one through train in each direction and connections at Doncaster for four others each way to and from the capital. The same important route also carried the service to Sheffield Victoria, to which six daily trains ran, with three express services running beyond to Manchester (London Road or Central) and Liverpool Central. Certain of the trains contained a dash of yellow and brown in the shape of a through coach for Swansea. A third interesting utilisation of the Staddlethorpe-Goole route was by the L&Y (LMS) services through Goole and Mirfield to Manchester Victoria and Liverpool Exchange, this time offering trains of handsome maroon and straw livery. The emigrant traffic from the Continent to America via Zeebrugge, Hull and Liverpool was served by connecting trains running round from Riverside Quay to Paragon to link up with the morning arrival and evening departure of the vessel. The LMS ran through coaches directly to the vessel from Liverpool. Extra services were provided between Hull and London, as now, by changing trains at Doncaster. Due to restriction placed on the use of the line by the Saltmarshe family, over whose land the Goole-Saddlethorpe line passed, there were on occasions, before the last war, no main line trains in operation on Sundays, a slender service being maintained by a steam railcar out to Doncaster. Sunday London passengers went via Selby where connections off the Leeds services were found, though there was a midday train from Hull which went straight through.

The Leeds service along the old run of the H&S numbered about twelve, of which three were through trains to Liverpool Lime Street via the LNWR, including the 9 a.m. which ran for many years and which was taken out by the Liverpool engine which had been stabled in Hull overnight. The 4 p.m. was also a 'crack' train hauled by a 'foreigner', sometimes a 'Prince of Wales'. Odd workings along the Leeds route were the slows to Selby only, certain trains which ran to York via Selby and Church Fenton, as they do today, and a fast early afternoon flyer from Hull to Pontefract via Selby which was reached on the average in 40 minutes. Reviewing the train services over some 80-90 years, it is difficult to register all the changes and one has to fall back upon an often inadequate general selection for atmosphere. However, the 3.20 p.m. from Hull is noteworthy in that it ran post-haste to Selby, then divided, the first half leaving at 4.05 p.m. for Sheffield which it reached at 5.19 a.m., a fine performance considering the route, the other portion setting out at 4.12 p.m. for Halifax, arriving at 5.25 p.m. For a period in the early 1900s several trains ran daily between Hull and Halifax, an experiment which was not repeated later, though for a time in the 1950s it was possible to travel by dmu directly to Bradford from Hull on weekdays via Morley High.

For many years a brisk local service ran out to Brough to serve the Blackburn Aircraft Works, later Hawker-Siddeley, which had established itself between the station and the river in the twenties. Push and pull sets hauled by small tanks or steam railcars would terminate here using the outside faces of the island platforms. In the later years of the service, trains of the rather

Probably a posed publicity shot for the introduction of the new H&BR corridor trains to Sheffield; No. 38 stands at Little Weighton; the first three coaches are all brake-compos (Collection C.T. Goode)

Ex-H&BR 0-6-0 No. 2418 on a local train at Hull Paragon station (T. Rounthwaite)

An A6 4-6-2T simmers gently on a local working for Hull at North Cave (C.T. Goode)

Ex-GC 2-8-0 brings a heavy eastbound freight up to the west of Drewton tunnel, H&B line (T. Rounthwaite)

nasty GN quintuple sets were used, hauled by the GC A5 4-6-2Ts which had seen much happier times in Marylebone. Today what is left of the local services is covered by stopping long distance trains at Brough, though not all do this as certain York and Leeds expresses run through non-stop. Ferriby and Hessle have lost all but a shadow of their early train services with none on Sundays. The four track section has been narrowed to two roads by the lifting of the Slow lines, and Hessle and Ferriby have had their platforms adjusted outwards to enable trains on the Fast lines to call. At the time of writing there are still three tracks running through Ferriby, the Up Slow surviving through the station to serve factories at Melton between there and Brough. A section of four tracks remains between Broomfleet and Staddlethorpe Jc. (Gilberdyke) which is needed on holiday Saturdays when there is a run of extra trains to and from Bridlington and Filey.

Staddlethorpe is the point of junction for the London and south and Leeds and west routes, and was extremely busy in its heyday, with two cabins at the Junction and East. The station itself is wooden and was unimportant locally until given a cause for existence by the building of a large housing estate at Gilberdyke, whereupon the name was changed and the station, still wooden, received a more important status.

An observer on the bridge here on a summer Saturday pre-war would have had a glorious time reviewing a whole range of motive power, even though much special traffic went by way of Selby and Market Weighton. Most of the former NER locomotive types would be seen on passenger trains running to Selby and Leeds, with various 4-4-0s of all ages hauling rakes of clerestory and non-corridor stock, D20s and the larger boilered D21s of Botanic Gardens shed with more impressive appearances by the C7 'Atlantics' in their pale green, and B16 4-6-0 mixed traffic engines, most of which seemed to have perpetual colds, to judge from the wheezing which beset them especially when recovering from a slack or starting off. These engines would appear on almost anything from fish trains to excursions, some of these being routed on the Slow roads from Staddlethorpe into Hull to give the main line to the 'regulars'.

Round the corner from Goole came a mixed bag of all sorts of engines. An LMS locomotive on a Wakefield-Hull off the L&Y system would be followed by a deep toned whistling, very staid and mild as one of the GC 'Directors', perhaps 'Worsley Taylor' from Sheffield's Darnall shed brought in an express from Liverpool Central complete with the carriage boards 'Liverpool-Sheffield-Doncaster-Hull', with no mention of Brough, Ferriby and Hessle, where almost all these trains stopped. Even leaving Hull the 4.13 p.m. to Liverpool Central managed the three stations and a homebound commuter living in Brough could, if he wished, and ate quickly, partake of afternoon tea which was served as soon as the carriage doors slammed at Paragon. 'Directors' clung to the Liverpool trains for many years, as did the smaller, beautiful D9s with their curving splashers. The morning 9.24 a.m. to Liverpoool Central was often a Hull turn and Botanic

Gardens turned out a D49 'Hunt' or 'Shire' 4-4-0 to work it to Sheffield, the locomotive returning on a lunchtime trip. This train was popular and often late and overloaded during the last war, so that a D20 or D17 was provided as pilot, particularly for the sharp bank out of Doncaster to Hexthorpe Jc. Quite often the train would stall here, especially with one of the old C7s or a D49 in poor shape. With a good load, setting back could not be resorted to and the whole assembly had to wait for succour. Sometimes Botanic Gardens would send out one of the GN 'Atlantics' which they had obviously had foisted upon them, grossly overrated engines and puny in comparison with the GC equivalents. On one occasion such an 'Atlantic' stalled and had to stand fuming until a J52 tank came out from Doncaster up the Goods line and was coupled up ahead of the ailing train. C1s were seen on 'The Yorkshire Pullman', usually of two or three coaches, proceeding briskly to Doncaster to join up with the Leeds portion there. After the last war a train ran ahead of the morning express to Liverpool Central, routed to Sheffield Midland via Swinton. This had good connections with the West Country, was sometimes extended to Birmingham and was always hauled by a D49, usually 'The Burton'.

The LNWR passenger workings of the thirties have already been mentioned; the goods equivalent was an LNW freight which would appear headed by one of the very plain looking 0-8-0 tender engines. Less plain and more spritely were the ex-NER goods engines of Class Q6 and the GC 2-8-0s which coped with the freight movements in all directions.

Our observer at Staddlethorpe, had he been on hand for a time around 1926 before the onset of the 'Sentinel' steam railcars, might have witnessed a real sight with the appearance of a converted Leyland bus operating from Selby shed, a 26-seater with rail wheels which ran in the area between Selby and Goole via Staddlethorpe and which, for a time, worked the Sunday link between Doncaster and the Leeds trains connecting at Staddlethorpe. The bus was destroyed by fire at Selby shed on Armistice Day 1926.

As the old faithfuls in the steam world were scrapped, so the variety available became less and runs were seen more and more behind D49s, the ubiquitous K3 2-6-0s and the all-purpose Thompson B1 4-6-0. Probably the last 'Director' to enter Hull on a passenger train was 'Marne' which left with the 4.13 p.m. to Liverpool Central on a happy day in 1958 when several of the class were kicking their heels on pilot duties at Sheffield Victoria. Apparently the rostered B1 had failed on leaving the shed and the crew had pleaded successfully to be allowed to take out No. 62670. The author was trying to teach a German class in a room upstairs in the old Boulevard School right next door to Anlaby Road crossing when one of his observant lads, a sympathetic member of the Railway Club raised his hand, bubbling over, and cried, 'Sir, a "Director" has just gone in!'. After the usual expressions of disbelief the report was believed. Yes, the coupling rod ringing had been unfamiliar, and no more work in 'Deutsches Leben' was done that afternoon.

The last operative passenger engines on the Humber bank were B1s, A5s and the V3 2-6-2 tanks, the latter getting a share of 'Yorkshire Pullman' duties. Ultimately the goods workings were left with the stalwart WD 2-8-0s which clanked on and on—and nobody seemed to take any notice of them until they had all faded away. Apart from the dwindling coal trains, a regular local WD duty was the transferring of chalk from the quarry at Hessle to Wilmington.

Trip workings around the yards were worked by the older and smaller engines, often the J72 tanks, and a special breed of big 4-8-0 tank lived at the Hump Yard for banking purposes. Dairycoates shed, about two miles west of Paragon station, was handily situated for the Riverside Quay and Fish Dock on the south side of the main running lines. To accommodate the increasing number of engines required for various duties, the shed was completely remodelled in 1913 and possibly the first mechanical coaling stage in the country, an affair of American appearance, was erected in 1916. The shed in its final form stabled 150 engines under cover and was about 380yd. by 130yd., making it the largest roundhouse of its type with six turntables and 130 radiating lines. Water was provided by the pumping house at Hessle. Botanic Gardens was the passenger sub-shed to Dairycoates which dealt with the trains out of Paragon, through Dairycoates handled a few passenger workings. However, freight runs were its main *raison d'être* and for the purpose it had ex NER engines of Classes B13-16 4-6-0s and the older 0-6-0s which were replaced eventually by the J39s which were virtually goods versions of the D49s. Ex GC 04 2-8-0s were also present, too, to work alongside the various NER 0-8-0s. For 'trip' workings round the docks, various 0-6-2Ts were available, as well as the larger A6 and A7 tanks. Largest of all were the above mentioned T1 4-8-0Ts used for hump shunting, while alongside them might be found the tiny Y8 0-4-0s. The classification letters are all of course post 1923.

Chapter 10

Into Holderness

Of the two lines running into Holderness towards the coast, the earlier was the Hull & Holderness Railway of 1854 which originally had its own engines and coaches, and which worked closely with the Y&NM running to the Victoria Dock station. In 1864, the year that the Hornsea Company came into being, the trains were diverted to run into Paragon station, taking the Victoria Dock branch round to the north of the city.

Considering the route of the Withernsea line first in its later years; this left the Dock branch near Great Union Street and was virtually flat for the whole of its eighteen miles and initially single throughout except for two sections, one between Hedon and Rye Hill, the other between Ottringham and Winestead, these being doubled in the early years of this century. In the vicinity of the timber sidings and adjacent to the busy Holderness road crossed on the level was Southcoates station, an island platform with a substantial building which would have been well placed to form an independent terminus for the line, had it survived. Turning eastwards the line found its way past various dockland lines, chiefly owing their existence to the later H&B, to run to the ancient township of Hedon via Marfleet, the latter station built to serve the village to the south and the expanding estate to the north of the line. Hedon station was conveniently situated to the north of the town and was a tablet station for entry to the single line section for Rye Hill. The track layout at Hedon was unusual in that both the Up and Down tracks came together short of the single platform, and that Hull-bound trains took a left curve to gain the correct line. The small yard was north of the platform, with the signal box at the level crossing.

Rye Hill village lay to the north of the station, Burstwick to the south, and here there were two platforms to serve each of the newly created Up and Down lines from the single track. Later additions to the complement of stopping places were Hedon Speedway Halt and Hedon Racecourse, the former being a shortlived idea of British Railways of 1948.

Although the terrain is flat, the line had to tack about a little where it encountered the 50ft. contour, and so Keyingham was set on a curve, the village being fairly close to it to the south. A short distance further to the east was Ottringham, again with its village to the south, though this time a mile away. At both stations the goods facilities were simple, Keyingham's yard being south of the station, Ottringham's to the north. Near each station were special sidings serving gravel pits, that at Kelsey Hill containing quite a decent run of industrial trackwork.

Beyond Ottrington the line became single once more and its course turned south, then east to avoid the wooded estates of Winestead and reach Patrington, a large village with a fine church called 'The Queen of Holderness', once the railhead for the wilder parts of the Holderness peninsula running east to Spurn Head.

Patrington station was conventiently placed at the west end of the village and next to the small gas works. Originally there was a station at Winestead, just to the west of Patrington, and traces of this survived to the end. In many ways the place had a greater potential than Patrington, with a brick and tile works and the Enholme Flax Mill south of the line. Winestead closed to passengers in 1904, but survived for freight until 1956.

From Patrington the line ran due north east through absolutely featureless scenery to its terminus at Withernsea, a small seaside town which owes much to the coming of the railway line which brought it a steady daily flow of happy trippers during the season, particularly from the poorer parts of East Hull through which the line passed, and also from the suburban stations of Botanic Gardens, Stepney and Wilmington, which were on the Victoria Dock branch running north of the city to Paragon station and which also served densely populated areas. The three stations were also common to Hornsea line trains, Botanic Gardens being fairly close to the sheds at a busy road junction and with the pleasure grounds to the left, a little out of view. Eventually the Botanic Gardens became Hymers College. West of the station was a complex of burial grounds which led whoever was responsible for such things to call the station 'Cemetery Gates' at first, hardly an inducement for anyone in the twilight of their days to purchase a single ticket! Botanic Gardens was a low single-storeyed building on the west side, with parallel platforms on a curve and some noteworthy North Eastern signals including a tall Up home. Stepney was a neat and dignified building on the south side towards the city and linked by the Beverley road trams which clattered over the level crossing. The signal box was on the opposite side of the crossing from the station, and managed to look as if it were an adjunct to the public house next door. From here loops on each side accompanied the line beneath the fine lattice girder bridge which brought H&B trains up from Cannon Street. To the east of this bridge on the south side was originally a station called Sculcoates which became a goods depot when the next station at Wilmington, an island platform in the style of Brough, was built in the early 1990s. The latter structure replaced two earlier stations, the second one being just round the corner on the Hornsea branch after it left the Victoria Dock line. Close by Wilmington station was a swing bridge over the river Hull, with a footpath alongside it. At the time of writing the footpath keeps the bridge from being dismantled and it has to be maintained for this simple right of way.

Withernsea station was basically an island with a main arrival platform on the north side and a recess at the outer end to form a second platform. The south side of the station also had a platform face, giving a total of three. The rail approach was somewhat ragged and complicated in an unnecessary way, departures fairing better as one could run straight out of the main platform without any fuss. The inner end of the main station road led on to a turntable from which the engine could be released by a run-round loop. On the south side were two long lines for the standage of rolling stock arrived on excursions, adjacent to the original Pleasure Gardens and Skating Rink of Victorian days.

Hornsea has always been regarded locally as slightly more elegant and less exciting than Withernsea. Probably these remarks are true even today, as there is less of the candy floss in Hornsea and more memorable things to find in the shape of a noted pottery and a large lake called the Mere. Hornsea is also slightly larger than Withernsea with around five and a half thousand residents.

The Hull & Hornsea Railway was a no-nonsense double line branch which ran in a generally north-easterly direction and managed to keep more or less level, reaching a height of no more than 66ft. throughout. In 1912, following the opening of the new Wilmington swing bridge, the branch really began at the newer Wilmington station. After the departure of sidings to the industrial site at Stoneferry, to the west, the first station encountered was Sutton-on-Hull with parallel platforms handily placed at the north west corner of the village, to be followed after a long reverse curve and a crossing of the Holderness Drain by Swine, placed at the east end of the village; although this is quite near to Hull, the place has only road access from the station end. The NER had virtually no choice in the naming of the station, as the only other village to hand was Coniston which would have caused fine confusion if it had been adopted. Swine station had staggered platforms with the yard on the Up side opposite the Down platform. Problems of naming came further along the line, however, with three stations within 1½ miles at Skirlaugh set well to the south of the village with its buildings on the north side adjacent to the level crossing with the main road, Ellerby and Burton Constable. Ellerby was closed in 1902 and was in fact equidistant from Ellerby village to the south east and Skirlaugh to the north west to which it was in fact closer than the official station of that name. Burton Constable, too, succeeded in serving nowhere in particular, being again about the same distance from Skirlaugh as the others and a good three miles from Burton Constable Hall to the south. The nearest small village here was Marton, not an inspiring name, and one which was more evocative of Blackpool than Holderness. The NER was unlucky enough to be saddled with a station called Constable Burton, a picturesque spot on the Hawes branch, so that Burton Constable had to go. One wonders how much freight and how many passengers were wrongly directed to either place!

Burton Constable station became Ellerby in 1922, reviving the name which had slumbered for twenty years. It was of course nowhere near Ellerby, but it provided the station staff there with the task of orientating any passengers as to their whereabouts on arrival. Both here and at Whitedale, the next station, the roadway crossed the line by a bridge.

Whitedale station was also interesting in that it was named after one house on the east side and not after the obvious choice of Rise Park on the other side, or even Withernwick to the east again. Possibly the nuns of Rise Convent might have upset the railway directors in this case, as an obvious choice was turned down. Here again the platforms were parallel and the yard on the east side was marginally larger than at the other roadside stations.

From Whitedale, which cannot have seen much traffic, the line ran almost northwards through stations at Goxhill and Wassand to Hornsea. Due to the well known station on the GN main line, as well to the presence of one of similar name on the GC near Doncaster, it was unwise to name a new station after the adjacent villages of Great and Little Hatfield, so that, again, the company had a dilemma and took instead the name Sigglesthorme from a village some three miles away.

It will be obvious by now that the Hull & Hornsea had an uneasy passage through Holderness as far as the nomenclature was concerned. The *coup de grace* came with Goxhill which was in direct conflict with another Goxhill on the south bank of the Humber which was served by the GCR. There was nothing at the Yorkshire Goxhill but a church; the name was tempting, however, and it was used until 1904 when it was changed to Wassand, named after a nearby Hall approached over a lengthy footpath. Wassand and its siding was closed in 1953, if one considers that it ever really opened, with one train each way for passengers shopping.

Hornsea was served by two stations, Bridge and Town, the former sited where the main road to the south passed beneath the line. Its buildings were at road level and ramps led up to the platforms. This station served Hornsea proper and on the north side were the coal drops and goods facilities. The station was very convenient for the Mere with its masts visible on the west side. A short run further on took holidaymakers to Town station, which was within the throw of a beach ball from the sea. It had an excellent run of buildings and a portico to heighten the sense of occasion on arrival. The station layout here was far simpler than that at Withernsea with a straight run in and out from the two parallel platforms, with an additional Down arrival platform and storage line and a short bay for departures on the Up side. A turntable of 46ft. 4in. diameter kept away all but the smaller engines. Water for them was obtained by means of a wind pump mounted on top of the storage tank. A scissors crossover at the entrance to the station neatly gave access to all four platform faces, and the brick signal box was on the departure side.

'The line will accomodate a great part of the rich and productive district of Holderness. It will bring the various markets of Yorkshire and Lincolnshire within reach of the agriculturist and enable him to send his cattle, grain and general produce to the best market, and to obtain lime, coal and other articles in return at a very considerably reduced price. The traffic in cattle, corn and other agricultural produce will be great. That from coal, lime, manures and gravel will prove a source of great revenue and a large market traffic may be anticipated.' So reads the Prospectus of the Hull & Hornsea Railway of 1852.

In the case of the two branches this seemingly optimistic forecast was generally proved correct, possibly the traffic received being greater than what was sent. Loads of manure were sent from Stepney Goods and stacked at Rye Hill station for farmers and mushroom growers. On the branches one station master would often be in charge of two or more stations, as Rye Hill & Burstwick which supervised Keyingham, and Skirlaugh which managed Ellerby, actually the busier station. The station master was thus kept quite busy with general duties, payment of wages, goods and passenger accounts and sending off of parcels. The hiring of sacks to local farmers was also quite renumerative. However, one business which was perhaps typically NER was the selling of coal by station masters who rented the coal drops, shovels, books and scales. The coal arrived at the station via an approved agent, loads being in wagons with bottom doors and payment made directly by the station master. In the 1950s the profit per ton was about 10/- before the payment of rents and hire charges. On taking over from a predecessor any coal stocks in the yard had to be paid for by his successor, and if much was left, then he could find himself with quite a large bill to pay. At some places coal sales were few; at Rye Hill the rentals totalled only £5 per annum. The principle of coal sales by station staff will no doubt go to explain why coal yards are often used as stations long after the sidings and in some cases the complete railway layout and access have been removed.

Goods train working on the branches consisted of pick-up runs on alternate days for each line, an old Class J 0-6-0 doing the honours. When loads bound for Hornsea Town were heavy and likely to cause problems up the climb to the road bridge, some of the vehicles were left at Whitedale for collection later. Passenger trains were worked by small 0-6-0 tender engines, but there was a later period when the old GN 4-4-2 tanks performed on both branches, to be superseded by the larger GC A5s.

'The number of passengers along the line will be very great, especially in the summer season. The German Ocean will be only about ¾ hour's run from Hull. The location of the Sea Terminus has been the subject of anxious consideration, and it is satisfying to state that the sands at Seathorn and Withernsea are excellent, and the approach thereto good and easy.' (The Prospectus again.)

Approximately thirteen trains ran between Hull and Hornsea in 1914, with the crack 8.50 a.m. businessmen's trains running non-stop over the 15½ miles in 28 minutes. A similar fast train left Hull at 5.18 p.m., taking the same time with conditional stops at Sutton and Hornsea Bridge. There were two trains each way on Sundays.

During the last war the service was cut back to nine trains each way, all of them slow and with a 'Sentinel' railcar running the two Sunday trains. By 1950 things had perked up, with a dozen trains each way and the restoration of an accelerated 8.50 a.m. Up and 5.18 p.m. Down. On Sundays there were now four trains each way including a fast working each way for day-trippers out of Hull. Wassand, it will be remembered, was allowed one service

Latterday pick-up goods at Little Weighton, with class B1 4-6-0 No. 61010 'Wildebeeste' (M. Haddon)

Sentinel railcar No. 272 "Hero" in wartime livery at Hull on 10 April 1946 (H.C. Casserley)

Class B1 4-6-0 No. 61276 awaits departure on the 12.12 p.m. to York, alongside a diesel set for Withernsea at Hull Paragon (C.T. Goode)

Class K3 2-6-0 No. 61875 crosses Anlaby Road with the Up 'Yorkshire Pullma (C.T. Goode)

The original Hull Paragon station entrance, now the parcels office (C.T. Goode)

Ex-H&BR 0-6-0 No. 2475 waits at Hornsea after arriving with an excursion (T. Rounthwaite)

A C12 class tank engine on a Hull train at Withernsea (C.T. Goode)

The 'Lincoln Castle' approaches Hull Corporation Pier (C.T. Goode)

each way per week. Until LNER days this was on Tuesdays by the 7.53 a.m. to Hull and off the 3.20 p.m. from the city. Then the day was changed to Monday, the trains being the 10.55 a.m. and 4.20 p.m. respectively. One wonders what harm would have been done by stopping the train daily.

On the Withernsea branch some twelve or thirteen trains ran in 1914 with a fast 8.20 a.m. train up to Hull which reeled off the 21 miles in 37 minutes. The return working was at 5.23 p.m., running into Withernsea at 6 p.m. Both services stopped at Southcoates for East Hull. There were also two trains each way on Sundays.

In 1940 the service was trimmed as on the Hornsea branch to nine trains, with the interesting exception that the 8.20 a.m. express continued to run, though with no balanced working out of Hull at teatime. Again, a 'Sentinel' operated the Sunday service.

In 1950 the service had recovered to roughly eleven trains each way daily, including the fast train to Hull, now at 8.18 a.m. with a return at 5.27 p.m. calling at Wilmington and Southcoates. On Sundays there were three basic slow trains and two high season fast services for excursionists.

Both branches were among the first to operate 'Paytrain' services with the then new dmus. Traffic levels were good, especially with casual holiday-makers who would stream on to the trains when the sun shone at the suburban stations. In 1950 it was still possible to go from Hull to Withernsea on a 2/- day return, and this really was a bargain.

Excursionists between the wars were ready to go anywhere, and it was possible for them to do so, especially if they were gregarious and clubbable. Just a few days taken from a summer week in 1925 are worth studying in detail to catch a glimpse of the sort of movement taking place on the two branches. For the purpose of our first observation we will go to Hedon on Saturday 11th July, where, in addition to the normal service of trains, a special No. 189 comes through at 8.50 a.m. made up of ten third class coaches plus brakes at each end, conveying the Courtney Street Baptist Sunday School party of 350 children and 200 adults from Southcoates which they had left at 8.38 a.m. They will have a good day and leave Withernsea at 7.20 p.m. Then, at 9.47 a.m., appears a real treat in the shape of a heavy train of six-wheelers and brakes, hauled by one of the recently acquired H&B domeless 0-6-0s carrying the special number 187. The engine puts up a spirited show as it gets away from Magdalen Gates after being checked because of the shunting of the pick-up goods which has been 'put inside' to let it pass. On board are a crowd of 750 youngsters and 290 adults from Dairycoates Wesleyan and Newington Parish Sunday Schools which have boarded at Hull, plus the Jubilee Sunday School party joined at Botanic Gardens en route. They will leave Withernsea at 8 p.m., tired but happy, and not a carriage will be found in any way damaged after the day is through. The pageant is completed by the passage of the third special at 9.58 a.m. after the pick-up has fled to Rye Hill. This is a train of the older L&Y coaches now in LMS maroon, hauled by an L&Y engine with very spartan cab arrangements, filled with miners and their families from Knottingley. They will leave the seaside at 8.30 p.m.

The second observation could be made on the Hornsea branch at the time of Hornsea Show on Thursday 16th July 1925 when the branch gained a substantial increase in traffic. One particular school special on this day was number 188 which left Hull at 8.15 a.m. made up of 13 small coaches and front and rear brake vans with children from the Albion Congregational, Parkin's and Park Street Unitarian Sunday School parties totalling 200 children and 60 adults, then taking up a further 250 children and 50 adults of the Lambert Street Primitive Methodist Sunday School party at Botanic Gardens. The party left Hornsea at 7 p.m.

To convey livestock from York, a special left there at 8.40 a.m., calling at all the principal stations to Hull and running express to Hornsea Bridge where it arrived at 11.30 a.m. The return was scheduled for 6.50 p.m.

Chapter 11

Abercrombie and Today

Hull was heavily bombed during the 1939-45 war, and even at the present time some of its scars are still visible. In 1946 it was possible to stand at the main entrance to Paragon Station and look out upon a scene of almost complete devastation and ruin particularly towards the south east. So it was that a report was drawn up for the City Council by Sir Patrick Abercrombie which included an interesting set of suggestions for the redevelopment of the railways within the city area. Basically the chief suggestion was to turn all trains entering the city on to the high level H&B railway and to penetrate the centre by way of the spur running down towards Cannon Street goods station with a slight deflection to a new terminus in Wright Street. Trains entering the city from the west already needed to climb over the dockland lines at Dairycoates, and this height could be maintained on a new spur round to the H&B branch to Neptune Street goods depot.

Improvident routing of the old railways without regard to future housing development which had to be fitted into the odd shapes of land that the lines had left afforded little hope of carrying out a massive re-planning in the future. So many ground level lines prevented whole areas of the city from being developed sympathetically with each other, and proliferated many level crossings, some of which were more often closed than open. The City Works and Tramway Committees of 1925 proposed the abolition of some lines and the elevating of others, while the LNER itself attempted to float a Bill in 1929 to empower them to construct new railways and abandon others. In the event the policy chosen was that of waiting until some lines were closed, then to construct two 'flyovers' over the worst offenders at Anlaby and Hessle Road crossings, a device which the Report considered makeshift and another way of dividing the community, as well as hampering the pedestrian. The principal crossings giving offence were as follows, the figures being taken during a census in January 1937:

	No. of trains in fifteen hours	*No. of times gates closed*	*Total times gates closed*
Hessle Road	191	120	5 hr. 42 min.
Anlaby Road	150	115	4 hr. 32 min.
Botanic Gardens	93	142	2 hr. 22 min.
Stepney	85	80	2 hr. 15 min.
Southcoates	62	56	1 hr. 45 min.

A schoolboy arriving late always had a good excuse—and there were always the river bridges!

On Springbank there were level crossings within a single mile and progress along its length on a holiday Saturday could be painfully slow.

Paragon station was to be phased out as new links were to be put in to

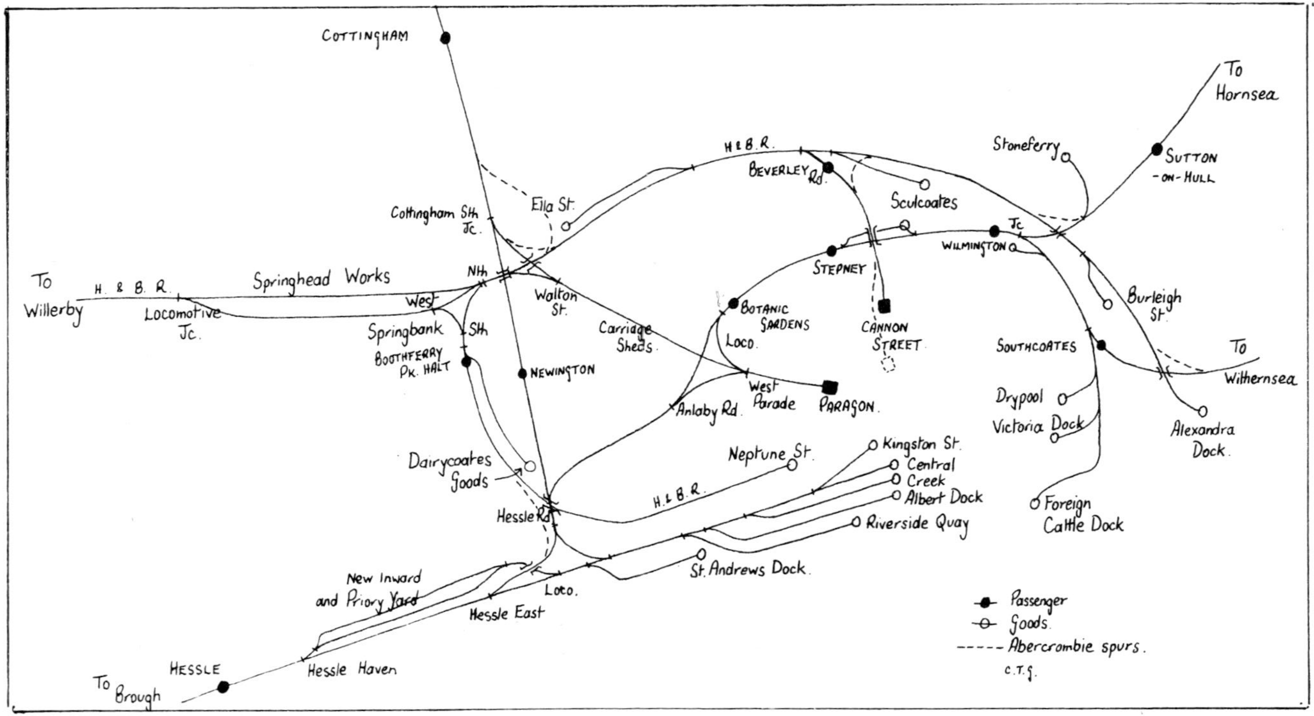
COTTINGHAM
To Hornsea
SUTTON -ON-HULL
Stoneferry
H & B. R.
BEVERLEY Rd.
Sculcoates
Ella St.
Cottingham Sth Jc.
Jc
WILMINGTON
STEPNEY
To Willerby
H. & B. R.
Springhead Works
Nth
Walton St.
West
Locomotive Jc.
Springbank
Sth
BOOTHFERRY PK. HALT
NEWINGTON
Carriage Sheds
BOTANIC GARDENS
Loco.
CANNON STREET
Burleigh St.
SOUTHCOATES
To Withernsea
West Parade
PARAGON
Anlaby Rd.
Drypool
Victoria Dock
Alexandra Dock
Dairycoates Goods
Neptune St.
Kingston St.
Central
Creek
Albert Dock
H. & B. R.
Hessle Rd.
Riverside Quay
Foreign Cattle Dock
St. Andrews Dock
New Inward and Priory Yard
Loco.
Hessle East
Passenger
Goods.
Abercrombie spurs.
C.T.G.
HESSLE
Hessle Haven
To Brough

convey the ground level lines to the H&B overhead route. The Station Hotel would be retained on site, while the electric signalling would be transferred (hopefully) to the new terminus.

As this new site would be quite near to the river Hull, it was hoped to increase the docking facilities here and construct sidings to serve them.

The hardest line to fit into the scheme was the Bridlington branch which required two new loops to cater for movements to and from the high level line. The branches to Hornsea and Withernsea were able to be accommodated by using spurs to the H&B line which ran close to them in the right places.

By adopting this plan the central area of the city would have been cleared of all level crossings and tidied up. Unfortunately the plan was not proceeded with, a compromise was resorted to and although much of the trackwork has vanished, Hull is left with two large bridges over the principal line out to the west and three level crossings, one of which, at Walton Street, can be a nuisance by virtue of its siting in relation to the roads around it and by the periods of heavy holiday rail traffic.

Like many other places Hull has been hit by the recession in industry and by the increasing amount of road usage preferred to the old rail facilities. Until the South Orbital road is completed, which will run parallel to the main line along the Humber bank from Hessle into the dockland area, there will be no real relief from the cavalcades of heavy lorries which noisily fill the city's main streets, most of them travelling to places directly served by rail and many of them carrying fish and timber, freight which used to be exclusively rail. The recession was partly brought about by the railways themselves when the Doncaster Division, under which the Hull area is organised, transferred coal and steel shipments to Immingham, and so found it possible to close various sidings and to reduce heavily the four-track section out to Staddlethorpe. Brough has lost its extra Down line and now has only two through platforms.

With a fairly low local car ownership there is a reasonably good use of passenger facilities, though as elsewhere local usage of buses is intense and preferred at Hessle, though in competition at Ferriby, Brough and Cottingham. At Beverley, too, the competition appears even with tickets interchangeable. Bridlington enjoys a regular clientele of rail users as the bus is slow, and there has never been an attempt to run an express road service here, surprising as the distance could be covered in the same time as the fastest train. Between Bridlington and Beverley the traffic is not great and most of the revenue comes in from the villages strung out along the Humber shore. Gilberdyke has, with renaming and astute publicity, enjoyed a 30 per cent increase in takings in two years, while Broomfleet is retained to cater for a village without a bus service. To their credit British Rail have on request improved the service at this little station which is unstaffed.

It is hoped that Brough will have a rosy future with the completion of the Humber Bridge, though for what reasons is not made clear. Certainly its building has not ruffled the railway calm apart from the use of the old

Priory Yard for the assembly of the decking sections. Brough handles 1,000 passengers per day and will soon have parking space for 250 cars. For pedestrians and the Cave villages it is badly placed, however, and some traffic is lost to the buses. Ferriby and Hessle soldier on with their regular customers and without any trains on Sundays. At Ferriby a bus which linked the station with other villages was reduced in evening frequency and was never consciously timed to connect with any trains arriving there. At Hessle, a bus which might offer a useful connection to Hornsea avoiding Hull, leaves from the village half a mile away and is infrequent. How many would use such a service is debatable, but no publicity has ever appeared co-ordinating rail and road.

Between Gilberdyke and Selby the three stations generate little traffic normally. Wressle has recently been officially de-staffed and Howden occasionally gains extra traffic when the Goole Bridge causes diversions and Goole passengers are transferred to rail there.

The Trans-Pennine units built in 1960 were regular performers in the area, originally running throughout between Hull and Liverpool via Huddersfield. For a time in the sixties one of the units would warm up by taking Armstrong Shock Absorber workers out to Beverley, then returning empty to take up station on the 9.40 to Liverpool. Later on troubles developed with the units which would often reach Leeds welcomed by swarms of fitters who would deliberate over some failure or other which had not been obvious earlier on the fast run through Standedge tunnel. The upshot was that odd driving units would be substituted, giving a ludicrous appearance to the set as a whole. Later policy cut back general workings to those between Hull and Leeds, passengers changing into Newcastle-Liverpool services. The preferred service became that to Manchester Piccadilly via Sheffield, a good one on which the Trans-Pennine units now run along with other Swindon built refugees from elsewhere.

From the beginning of 1981 the High Speed Train has been introduced into the King's Cross service, running in the path of the 'Hull Executive'. On its inaugural run conveying local worthies, the splendour was somewhat tarnished at Brough where some 60 passengers waiting to board found the doors locked, as the train had started from a right hand platform face at Paragon. Much work still remains to be done to bring the shaky stretch of line between Thorne Jc. and Doncaster up to a reasonable standard.

Principal London services were headed by 'Deltics' in many cases, the first, the 'Hull Executive' at 7.00 a.m. being too early for many people, though it gave an arrival in the Capital at a little before ten. The next departure for London passengers was at the more civilised time of 8.20 a.m. which was actually a Manchester Piccadilly service with a change for main line passengers at Doncaster. This service could become overloaded especially on holiday Saturdays. For many years a through train for London left Hull at the acceptable time of 8.47 a.m., followed by an equally decent timing to Leeds and beyond at 9.0 a.m. These two departures became the 9.36 and

9.53. The 9.36 was nearly always 'Deltic' hauled and something of a penance for these fine machines as they dragged the train along on and off the slow road to let HSTs past, and with stops in unlikely places which, however, produced many passengers. At Doncaster it was possible for the athletic and unencumbered to join an HST which hurled one to London much quicker. If this HST were late, then the 9.36 would be late as well and all its connections delayed, the effect rebounding throughout the Midlands and East Anglia.

Doncaster has always been a bone of contention as far as Hull travellers are concerned, and the attitude is much as it always was towards 'the branch' or 'poor relation'. Many are the passengers who have arrived at Doncaster to find that their connection has just left with no attempt to hold, while Cleethorpes units seem to wait about interminably. One reason for this is possibly that the Hull crews are working home, so anxious to be away, while Cleethorpes workings are often Doncaster-manned.

There are one or two services from Hull to York via Church Fenton, notably the 9.44, otherwise a change must be made across the bridge at Selby.

With opening of the M62 and M18 motorways, the railway has had to look to its laurels, as there are some smart National Bus services giving a good and cheap ride to Leeds via Wakefield, an important place which is virtually inaccessible by rail from Hull. A city hard to reach by rail from Hull is Nottingham, which at one time in the early sixties enjoyed a most interesting working in the shape of a two-car set which ran from Nottingham Midland with stops at Pye Bridge for some reason, Chesterfield, then to Sheffield and Hull with normal stops. This left at 9.00 a.m. and there seems to have been no corresponding working in the opposite direction.

Nottingham can be reached via Grantham, a dearer route than via Sheffield, where for many years the obvious trains by which any normal day tripper might go just did not connect there, one leaving two minutes before the other arrived. Similarly it was not possible to reach Lincoln to enjoy a full day as the connection had just left at Doncaster. Meanwhile the bus operators ran a daily express service to Nottingham from Hull in reasonable time at cheaper fares, and also served a town which the railway had written off years ago, Mansfield.

Immediate developments in the passenger field on Humberside should concentrate on strengthening the passenger links between Hull and Beverley and also Brough. Cottingham has enjoyed an expansion of trade and the car park there can store up to 60 vehicles. An interesting 'odd' station in the area is that at Boothferry Park, a single platform on the old Hull & Barnsley line, built to serve the football ground on a route handy for the running of diesel units to and from Paragon or for dealing with the arrival of special trains. The route also forms a handy diversionary link from Walton Street to Hessle Road should any blockage take place on the direct line. The latter has now lost its two major level crossings at Hessle and Anlaby Road to road bridges. The other crossings, at St. George's Road and Chalk Lane have barriers and are monitored by TV 'eyes' from the Hessle Road power box. The total number of manned level crossings for the area was high at 75, with a mere twelve bridges.

A second 'odd' station is the halt at Melton between Ferriby and Brough which serves the nearby factories, used by certain units which call there at the beginning and end of day shifts, and which is not publicly advertised outside the immediate area.

One closure, in spite of 15,000 passengers annually, was Filey Camp station, with its traffic now transferred to the Town station. Both Filey and Hunmanby were growth areas and had experienced an increase in rail traffic to and from Scarborough. Some savings had resulted from singling 11 miles of track between Hunmanby and Bridlington.

Attempts were made to close the Hull-Scarborough route in 1968 and surveys of passenger usage were carried out during the previous year in order to provide evidence at a public enquiry held in Bridlington, this during the following July. This was well attended and objections were heard from many quarters, most of them neatly parried by British Railways. Possibly it was the smaller places such as Arram which saved the line, though not the stations at Carnaby, Burton Agnes and Lowthorpe. Arram is two miles from the main road and the nearest bus, has only one bleak and circuitous way in or out and neither post office, shops or a doctor; in short, it had an unanswerable case for the retention of its railway service. At the time of the enquiry the author noted with regret that apart from himself and a handful of others, nobody else had travelled to the meeting by rail.

The line's future seems fairly safe and two good summers brought a boom in casual holiday travel with extra trains of loco hauled stock required and a possible peak on a June Sunday in 1975 when 17 specials arrived at Bridlington, shades of the old steam days. Non-stop trains operated in summer covering the 31 miles in 38 minutes. Although this is all too often a bad sign, many of the stations have been repainted and gardens restocked. Beverley used to be a regular winner of the Station Garden contests, along with Burton Agnes. A local group including some railwaymen is exploring the possibility of re-opening part of the former Hull-Hornsea route from Sutton, near which is Hedon and the large housing estate of Bransholme.

Freight traffic, particularly in small wagon loads, has suffered. Many acres of land have been cleared of the old yards, four large ones having disappeared in the past decade. The Western Docks are no longer rail-connected and both the fish and timber traffic go by road. The Eastern Docks, however, are still linked by what is left of the old H&B 'overhead line' with colour light signalling and up-graded track to the junction at Hessle Road. Over it passed some 200,000 tons of chemicals from the great names in oil refining at Saltend, out in block loads to places such as Spondon, Baglan Bay and Stockton.

About ten per cent of the shipping cargo was retained by rail from the

King George and Alexandra Docks, with loads of bauxite and steel, both imported and exported, and mail. The bauxite was processed locally, and moved a further stage by rail to Stafford and Welwyn.

There is activity west of the city, primarily from the adapted New Yard with its 23 sidings to cater for some local and trunk services bringing loads to West Yorkshire, Tinsley and Scunthorpe. A 'catch' for rail was made two or three years ago when Tilcon set up a plant at Dairycoates to process limestone for building contractors which was brought in block loads from Rylstone on the old Grassington branch near Skipton, each train headed by two Class 25s. The distinctively labelled hopper wagons brought a total of 230,000 tons of material per year.

North of the line to the west of the city can be seen the Freightliner depot, from which point ran a daily service to Leeds where goods can be forwarded to Glasgow and London. Other block trainloads convey steel goods, bricks, salt and continental ferry traffic. Presflow vans were found at the cement works at Melton, while near here too is the smelting plant of Capper, Pass to which tin ore traffic ran from Avonmouth. The only other significant traffic currently of note was the circuit working of 19 wagons which left Beverley conveying whiting from a local firm to paper mills in Aberdeen. During the past five years the shape of the railway system in the East Riding has hardly changed at all and is likely to remain so for several years to come.

There were three minor railways in East Yorkshire. These have not been covered here as all have had detailed books written about them. There was the Derwent Valley Railway, a standard gauge line opened on 29 October 1912 from Cliffe Common to Wheldrake and to York (Layerthorpe) on 21 July 1913. Passenger traffic ceased on 1 September 1926, but the line remained open for goods, being progressively shortened, and is now closed from York to Dunnington. The Spurn Head Railway, another standard gauge line unconnected with any other ran from Kilnsea out to the Point, being opened about 1910, closed 1951, and mostly used by coastguard men and military. Finally, the Sand Hutton Railway opened on the 15-inch gauge in the grounds of Barnby House in 1912, and in 1922 was relaid to the 18-inch gauge and opened publicly from Warthill NER station to Bossall; passenger traffic began on 4 October 1924, but the line closed entirely in 1932.

Chapter 12

The Humber Ferry

Part of the Humberside transport scene was the ferry which plied across the estuary from Hull Corporation Pier to New Holland on the south bank, and although not strictly a railway, nevertheless this particular operation was for many years carried out under the railway aegis and was run from 'the other side'. One of the recent delights of wandering in Hull was to turn down towards the river and to see a plume of black smoke rising above the old warehouses, then to turn into Nelson Street by the riverside and find oneself in what could well be Flemish or Dutch atmosphere created by the trees and the style of the buildings themselves. The station building was definitely 'foreign' and had the initials 'MS&LR' on it, representing the company across the water. Not many stations existed selling tickets without a nearby train to catch. Until its removal in the fifties the elevated iron promenade over the jetty gave the area an additional foreign flavour. The smoke came, of course, from the *Lincoln Castle*, the last and youngest survivor of the three paddle steamers which together used to maintain the service from the year of *Lincoln Castle*'s construction in 1940, thus all through the last war.

The Humber has been an obstacle of forty miles in length from time immemorial, causing the Romans to construct the first ferry from Winteringham to Brough as part of the Ermine Street which ran from Lincoln to York. Then Canute the Dane set up a ferry between North and South Ferriby; subsequently the southern terminus was moved to Barton. Edward I who virtually established Kingston-upon-Hull, crossed from Barton to Hessle with the City's new charter. He was obviously impressed by his crossing, as in 1316 his son Edward II granted another charter to the City to allow them to operate in perpetuity a ferry between Hull and Barton, pedestrians being charged one halfpenny, horsemen one penny and so on.

The ferry existed for many years and in 1640 we hear of the poet Andrew Marvell's father being drowned in the Humber while making a crossing. Footpads and highwaymen caused a diversion of the road approaching the ferry to be made through Brigg to Barton.

As well as running the gauntlet of Lincolnshire cut-throats, travellers had to put up with a ferry crossing which often took up to eight hours. This was reduced to 1½ hours in the early nineteenth century when the family which owned the ferry put on 'sloop-rigged' packets which were met by stage coaches at each end.

The fifth crossing and most easterly came with the railways when the run from New Holland was opened in 1848. There is some evidence that an earlier form of ferry had existed linking Hull to New Holland, a form of do-it-yourself affair with luckless passengers having to wield their oars like galley slaves. Much relief, therefore, when the MS&L Company built and opened their 1,500ft. jetty at New Holland for the expeditious handling of passengers and freight at all states of the tide. The pier is noteworthy as the early work of Sir John Fowler who designed the Forth Bridge. A floating pontoon at New Holland vanished during a storm in 1869. The railway to Grimsby was of course opened at the same time and steam vessels were brought from the Gravesend Steamboat Company. The first paddle steamer built for the service was the *Manchester* of 1849, followed by the *Liverpool* of 1855 and she had eight successors up to the Great War. The later vessels, the *Cleethorpes* of 1903 and the *Brocklesby* and *Killingholme* of 1912 were requisitioned by the Admiralty for naval services at this time and two smaller vessels stood in for them. *Cleethorpes* built by Gourlay Bros., looked like a normal paddle steamer and was 190ft. long by 25ft. The other two were built by Earles of Hull, were 195ft. long by 31ft. wide, had a greater draught at 8ft. 6in. and were double ended. Their tall funnels spoiled their appearance.

A floating pontoon was provided at the Hull Victoria Pier in 1901, but this sank in a gale in 1916. Relief from the steep, narrow and often slippery approach ramps had to come eventually, and in 1936 the approaches were modernised and pontoons provided at both ends of the ferry, each 150ft. by 50ft., connected by 23ft. wide bridges with a ten foot roadway and two flanking paths each of five feet. At high water the hinged approaches were roughly level, steepening to 1 in 9 at low tide. On 22nd. December 1934, in advance of the alteration, two new paddle steamers, the *Wingfield Castle* and *Tattershall Castle* arrived from the shipyard of Messrs. Gray of West Hartlepool, each name complimenting Hull and Lincolnshire respectively. Wingfield Castle in Suffolk was the seat of the De La Pole family, merchants of Hull.

At the time of their inauguration much was made of the buffet facilities on board, and of the improved space for passengers and the comfort offered to them. A third vessel, the *Lincoln Castle*, was put on the service in 1940. Of similar design, she had the same dimensions, apart from being two feet shorter.

The war years and the growth of post-war traffic began to take their toll of the familiar paddle steamers which did valiant work in all weathers across a tricky river with its shifting sands capable of holding a vessel fast for several hours, as happened fairly often. The service was normally maintained by two vessels, the third being moored at New Holland upstream of the pontoon, either being serviced or spruced up for a Sunday run to Grimsby.

The first vessel to go was the *Tattershall Castle* in 1972, to become a floating art gallery on the Thames, followed by the *Wingfield Castle* in 1974, for which a replacement was found in the shape of the *Farringford*, built in 1947 and transferred from the Isle of Wight service. She was a diesel electric paddle vessel and virtually a superior kind of military landing craft adapted for side loading at the pontoons. Accommodation was quite good and totally enclosed, with no areas of upper deck to wander about on as with the 'Castles'. *Farringford*'s chief disadvantages were her deep draught which could send her on a long detour down towards the eastern docks to avoid the shallows, also the presence of bow spray washing cars on board when the water was choppy. However, her capacity was almost twice that of her steam companion.

The *Lincoln Castle* was popular with enthusiasts during her last years of operation, and when working with *Farringford* it was she who had the privilege of connecting with the rail service to and from Barton and Grimsby. If one vessel were out of action for servicing or for any other reason, then it was possible for one vessel to cover all sailings, some twenty or so per day, by smart turn-rounds. When it was clear that her days were numbered, a group of enthusiasts made efforts locally to preserve *Lincoln Castle* as a working venture, but unfortunately neither local enterprise nor the National Railway museum were able to help materially, and the vessel was laid up for a period before being purchased by a local restaurateur who wished to moor it opposite his waterfront premises. This was not possible and now the *Lincoln Castle* lies high and dry just below the Humber Bridge on Hessle foreshore, in use as a restaurant and gradually being restored from the interior outwards.

A period of uncertainty ensued for *Farringford* and its staff, while the opening date of the Humber Bridge was deferred from week to week. This was phrased thus in the official closure notice:

'With the anticipated opening to traffic of the new suspension bridge across the Humber in early June 1981, Sealink UK Ltd hereby gives notice that its passenger vehicular service between Hull Corporation Pier and New Holland Pier will cease to operate from Sunday 7th June 1981 with the scheduled arrival of the *Farringford* at Hull Corporation Pier on completion of the last sailing from New Holland Pier on that date. In the event of the anticipated bridge opening date being further delayed beyond the 7th June, Sealink will make every effort to continue to operate the ferry service until such time as the bridge is open to traffic. A connecting rail service will operate to and from New Holland Pier pending the bridge opening.'

Meanwhile the ferry attracted many people who suddenly realised that it existed and who took advantage of a special cheap fare offered during the final days. The Bridge opened at noon on Wednesday 24th June and the last through ferry service from Hull connecting with the train to Cleethorpes was the 10.30 which served the 11.30 train. Thereafter the trains ran to and from the Barton branch, calling at a newly opened halt at New Holland on the south side of the triangular layout near the site of the old engine shed.

The last service runs by *Farringford* were the 18.15 from New Holland and 19.30 back from Hull on that day, for which £2.50 return ticket was charged. At the time of writing the Humber Bridge is proving a popular attraction by its novelty and is indeed an imposing piece of engineering. There is no doubt, however, that it will not rouse the transport enthusiast or give the same pure pleasure to the discerning traveller that the ferry did.